ACPL ITEM
DISCARDED

POLICY PAPERS

NUMBER 30

THE ECONOMIC CONSEQUENCES
OF THE PERSIAN GULF WAR:
ACCELERATING OPEC'S DEMISE

ELIYAHU KANOVSKY

THE WASHINGTON INSTITUTE FOR NEAR EAST POLICY
WASHINGTON, D.C.

Library of Congress Cataloging-in-Publication Data

Kanovsky, Eliyahu.
    The Economic Consequences of the Persian Gulf War: Accelerating OPEC's Demise / Eliyahu Kanovsky.
        p. cm. – (Policy Papers / The Washington Institute for Near East Policy ; No. 30)
        ISBN 0-944029-18-3 : $11.95
        1. Petroleum industry and trade. 2. Iraq-Kuwait Crisis, 1990-1991—Economic aspects. 3. Middle East—Economic Conditions.
        I. Title. II. Series: Policy Papers (The Washington Institute for Near East Policy) ; No. 30.
    HD9560.5.K36 1992
    338.2'3282—dc20   92-13613
                                             CIP

Cover design by Jill Indyk

THE AUTHOR

Eliyahu Kanovsky is professor of economics at Bar-Ilan University in Israel and is the Ludwig Jesselson Visiting Professor of Economics at Yeshiva University in New York. He is the author of numerous economic studies, including *Another Oil Shock in the 1990s? A Dissenting View* (1987) and *Opec Ascendant? Another Case of Crying Wolf* (1990) both published by The Washington Institute for Near East Policy.

CONTENTS

ACKNOWLEDGEMENTS

As the Ludwig Jesselson Visiting Professor of Economics at Yeshiva University, New York, I have benefitted greatly from the cooperation of the university, and in particular, the Mendel Gottesman Library, in the preparation of this study. I am especially grateful to Mr. Ludwig Jesselson.

At Bar-Ilan University, Israel, thanks are due to many, but especially to Mrs. Sylvia Sack and to Gilda Wohl for their patient typing and, often retyping, of the accompanying statistical tables—the building blocks of the study.

At The Washington Institute for Near East Policy, Yehudah Mirsky and Ellen Rice have done an excellent job of editing.

Finally, the forebearance and encouragement of my wife Tamar, my children and grandchildren, made it possible for me to devote myself to this study.

LIST OF ABBREVIATIONS

MBD	Millions of barrels per day
TBD	Thousands of barrels per day
GNP	Gross National Product
GDP	Gross Domestic Product
UAE	The United Arab Emirates
MEED	*Middle East Economic Digest*
MEES	*Middle East Economic Survey*
EIU	Economist Intelligence Unit
IMF	International Monetary Fund

PREFACE

Of the many strategic interests that the United States and its allies have in the Middle East, surely one of the most crucial is securing energy supplies from that region. The Gulf War of 1991 demonstrated, if nothing else, the importance of Middle East oil in the world community's strategic calculus. Since the oil shocks of the 1970s, much attention has focused on the Organization of Petroleum Exporting Countries (OPEC); indeed, much of the influence that Arab, and particularly Gulf, states have wielded in world affairs derives from their asserted cohesiveness and presumed ability to bring the industrialized world to its knees with a turn of the spigot.

This widely-held belief rests on two assumptions: that oil is and will continue to present a seller's market in the foreseeable future, and that the countries comprising OPEC will pursue common policies toward common objectives. In this Paper, Eliyahu Kanovsky, a distinguished and veteran analyst of the economics of Middle Eastern oil, argues that both these assumptions are false—that for a variety of reasons the price of oil will most likely drop in the near future. He postulates that the countries of OPEC will, as they have in the recent past, pursue their own interests, which has usually meant selling as much oil as they can, and in the process dilute their political strength. This pattern, he argues, was set in motion well before Saddam Hussein's invasion of Kuwait. The events following August 2, 1990, then, have merely served to reinforce and accelerate the process.

Professor Kanovsky's analysis has profound implications for policymakers around the world—and especially in the

U.S., as it reassesses American strategic priorities in the post-Cold War era. This Policy Paper is a timely contribution—as it charts significant trends that have been in motion for some time and will likely continue into the future, with implications for the health of the world's economy and the potential for conflict in the future.

Barbi Weinberg
President
August 1992

EXECUTIVE SUMMARY

This study aims to assess the **longer term** economic impact of the Persian Gulf War and its aftermath on oil markets generally, and on a number of Middle Eastern countries affected by the crisis. As compared with 1973-74 and 1979-80, this was a "mini oil shock."

Saudi Arabia has been incurring large budgetary and balance of payments deficits since 1983. The Saudis' postwar decision to double their armed forces and to acquire far more sophisticated military equipment will exacerbate their long-term financial problems. Experience has taught them that a sharp price hike will inevitably be followed by a bust and a longer term reduction in oil demand. Their most vital national interests dictate opposition to significant oil price increases. Instead, they will aim to acquire a bigger share of the market.

While Saudi Arabia and other Middle East oil exporters were incurring deficits during most of the 1980s, Kuwait's budgetary and balance of payments surpluses, though diminished, continued to be positive. But war-related expenditures have reduced Kuwaiti assets, and reconstruction costs will drain them further. Its dependence on oil revenues is far greater than before the war, and it will seek to expand production as rapidly as possible. Kuwait ignored OPEC quotas in the past and is even more likely to do so in the future.

The war against Iran (1980-1988) left Iraq impoverished, it had exhausted its financial reserves, and despite considerable aid from the rich Arab states, it incurred huge debts to European countries, the U.S. and others. The seizure of Kuwaiti assets and oil revenues was seen as a quick cure. Instead, the war left Iraq even more destitute. No one can predict when sanctions will be lifted, but when they are, Iraq may be expected to utilize its enormous oil potential to expand exports beyond prewar levels. It will not be restrained by OPEC quotas.

Iran was not directly involved in the Persian Gulf War, but it is still suffering from the aftermath of the 1979 revolution and its eight-year war with Iraq. It is expanding oil production capacity as rapidly as possible to meet its pressing need for cash.

During the crisis, fully one half of the shortfall arising from the cessation of Iraqi and Kuwaiti oil exports was offset by expanded Saudi production, and the balance by Venezuela, Iran, the United Arab Emirates, Libya, Nigeria and Indonesia, as well as Mexico and other non-OPEC producers. Most of these are planning significant expansions of productive capacity, while new producers worldwide are entering the market. Most Third World countries now welcome Western oil companies, whose capital resources and advanced technology enhances the likelihood of discoveries. The Gulf War itself has given new impetus to exploration, especially outside the Middle East.

Egypt's economy was in terrible shape before the war: Gross National Product (GNP) and incomes were declining; oil revenues and remittances from Egyptians working in the Gulf states were falling; inflation and unemployment were rising; and payments due on the debt were unbearable. More fundamentally, three decades of adverse economic policies had stimulated consumption and hampered production and efficiency. In 1991, under pressure from the International Monetary Fund, Egypt undertook painful economic reforms— strongly opposed by powerful interest groups—but the record of past commitments to reform does cast doubt on the present program. The massive dose of foreign aid during the Gulf War not only gives Egypt a reprieve, it also enables the leadership to avoid biting the bullet.

During most of the 1980s there was a steady deterioration in Syria's economy and living standards fell precipitously. To make matters worse, following the invasion of Kuwait over 100,000 Syrians were expelled. On the other hand, Syria had the good fortune of finding a major oil field in its north east, and since the late 1980s production has been rising rapidly. The higher oil prices since the Persian Gulf War have added to Syria's good fortune. It also received considerable funds from the rich Gulf states—a reward for its support of the war effort—which according to press reports have enabled Syria to augment its arms imports. Much of the currently projected growth in the volume of Syrian oil exports, however, will be offset by lower prices. If history is any guide, following the oil boom, Syria's economy will again revert to stagnancy.

Through the 1980s, Jordan's economy was going from bad to worse: GNP was declining; incomes and living standards were rapidly deteriorating; inflation and unemployment were rising; and in 1988 Jordan defaulted on debt payments. The Persian Gulf War exacerbated the situation, especially since Jordan was punished for siding with Saddam Hussein. Arab aid ceased; U.S. aid was suspended; and following the liberation of Kuwait almost all its Palestinians-Jordanians, about 300,000, were expelled. However, Japan and some European countries have given Jordan over $1 billion, and it appears that U.S. aid will be reinstated. Nonetheless, even if economic growth is resumed, it is difficult to see a long-term solution for the very large number of unemployed—most of whom are university graduates. As a result, the social and political stability of Jordan may well be undermined.

The continued decline in production and exports of the former USSR has been a major factor in sustaining oil prices since the Persian Gulf cease-fire. However, CIS's oil potential has hardly been scratched. New policies welcoming foreign investment will probably bring a turnaround within the next few years.

The oil shocks of the 1970s gave a powerful boost to improvement in overall energy efficiency and fuel-switching away from oil. In recent years governments have taken stronger measures to reduce pollution, including the increasing displacement of oil by environmentally cleaner natural gas. Moreover, natural gas reserves are growing more rapidly than oil reserves, and their costs are lower.

In all, the outlook for the 1990s is for a slow growth in oil demand and a more rapid growth in available supplies, which will tend to depress prices, at least when measured in constant (inflation-corrected) dollars. The Persian Gulf War gave a further boost to those forces which restrain demand and increase supplies. Prices will be even more depressed when Kuwait and Iraq fully reenter the market. Notwithstanding price fluctuations arising from weather, accidents, wars, revolutions and the like, the underlying trends point to lower prices. As a result, **OPEC's power to control prices will be even weaker than in the past**.

For the oil-importing countries—rich and poor—lower oil prices will be a blessing, reducing inflation, lowering interest rates, and stimulating economic growth, jobs and incomes. But for those countries heavily dependent on oil, problems may multiply, since one-crop economies are inherently weak, and oil is no exception. The political power of OPEC will, accordingly, further decline.

INTRODUCTION

The Persian Gulf War, which for our purposes can be said to have begun with Iraq's invasion of Kuwait in August 1990 and ended with Iraq's expulsion nearly seven months later, wrought many changes—political, strategic and economic. Many of these changes will be long-lasting. The focus of this paper is on the longer term economic ramifications for oil markets and for the economies of a number of Middle Eastern states.

In some respects, the impact of the Kuwait crisis was similar to that of the oil shock of the 1970s—though much smaller in magnitude. The oil shock of 1973-74 raised prices from about $3 per barrel to $10-11 per barrel, and the oil shock of 1979-1980 hiked prices to almost $40 per barrel. During the 1970s and early 1980s, the major oil-exporting countries enjoyed what appeared to be almost unlimited prosperity, while oil-importing countries suffered economic stagnation, unemployment and inflation. The overwhelming majority of oil analysts had projected an almost continual rise in prices during the 1980s and beyond. However, the reaction of the market was swift, powerful and almost totally unexpected. Oil prices peaked in 1981, and though there were fluctuations—as with the prices of other commodities—the overall trend was distinctly and strongly downward from a peak of nearly $40 per barrel in 1981 to about $14 in June 1990. **Measured in constant dollars (i.e., corrected for dollar inflation), prices in mid-1990 (before the Gulf crisis) were back to their levels of 1973-74.**

One of the crucial assumptions of oil forecasters in the 1970s was that the major oil-exporting countries in the Middle East, with their small populations, were "small absorbers" of revenues. In other words, they did not have the "absorptive capacity" to spend all or most of the flood of oil revenues. This assumption led to the conclusion that Saudi Arabia, and other major exporters with small populations, would continue to accumulate huge financial reserves. Numerous scholars addressed themselves to the anticipated problem of "recycling" the huge and growing OPEC financial surpluses. From the point of view of world oil markets, the implication was that the OPEC cartel had unusual strength, since any temporary oil glut which threatened to lower prices could easily be offset by a reduction in oil output on the part of Saudi Arabia and other major small-population oil-exporters, who in any case, it was argued, could not absorb the inflow of oil revenues.

The reality proved to be entirely different. **Since 1983, Saudi Arabia and other large Middle East oil exporters have been incurring deficits in both budgets and balance of payments (the current account) and have been unwilling to reduce oil output significantly in order to raise or even sustain oil prices.** The precarious financial situation of many members of OPEC, as well as other factors, exert strong pressure on those countries with unutilized productive capacity to increase their output, even if it is in violation of OPEC agreements. In the 1980s, Saudi Arabia and other major oil exporters with small populations began to compete with other producers, in or out of OPEC, for a greater share of the market. Moreover, even before the Kuwait crisis, many oil producers in the Middle East and elsewhere had announced plans for a large-scale expansion of capacity and some were implementing these plans. Saudi Arabia, which had produced 5.2 million barrels a day (MBD) in 1988 and again in 1989, had announced plans to expand capacity to 10 MBD. These efforts, both Saudi and others, have intensified since the crisis.

Toward the end of the 1980s, and especially in 1989 when oil prices were rising, the prevailing view among oil analysts was that the 1990s would see a resurgence in oil prices. (These forecasts were based on an analysis of the *economic* factors affecting oil markets, not on the expectation of a political-military crisis.) The present author, in a paper published in 1990, before the invasion of Kuwait, expressed a dissenting view that long-term oil prices were heading downward, at least when measured in constant dollars.[1] The sharp decline in oil prices during the first half of 1990 (before the Iraqi invasion) seemed to indicate, in retrospect, that the 1989 price hikes were, for the most part, due to a constellation of unforeseen, temporary factors, including accidents in the North Sea, the Exxon Valdez debacle in Alaska and unusual weather conditions in North America and Europe. During the first half of 1990 these special factors had, for the most part, expended themselves, and prices declined to their 1988 levels, measured in nominal dollars (and even lower in constant dollars).

The "mini" oil shock wrought by the Kuwait crisis, aided by the sharp decline in Soviet oil output, raised prices to about $40 per barrel in September 1990. This was soon followed by an almost steady decline to about $20-25 per barrel. The shape of the longer-term reaction will be similar to that which occurred after the earlier major oil shocks. **During the course of this decade, prices, at least when measured in real dollars, will be even lower than what they might have been in the absence of the 1990-91 crisis.** If this projection is reasonably accurate, this will have important ramifications for oil markets in general, and for Middle Eastern economies, in particular.

---

[1] See Eliyahu Kanovsky, *OPEC Ascendant? Another Case of Crying Wolf,* Policy Paper No. 20, (Washington, D.C.: The Washington Institute for Near East Policy, 1990).

I SAUDI ARABIA

1973-83—THE YEARS OF PLENTY

Saudi budgetary policies offer a classic example of expenditures chasing revenues and then overtaking them. The 1973-74 oil shock raised government revenues (overwhelmingly from oil) from $4 billion in 1972-73 to $28 billion in 1974-75. A five-year plan was adopted which called for total public expenditures of $142 billion, almost seven times actual spending in the previous five years (measured in current dollars). In the mid-1970s the conventional wisdom among foreign analysts was that the Saudis could not possibly spend sums even approaching these figures, and hence, they forecast large and continued financial surpluses. The main categories of expenditures specified by the plan included massive allocations for infrastructure, educational and health and other social services, housing and urban development, the establishment of modern industry (and, to some extent, agriculture), as well as large-scale military spending.

Though revenues continued to rise, a budgetary deficit emerged in 1977-78 followed by an even larger deficit in the following year. Meanwhile, massive government spending provided a powerful stimulus to the economy and imports of both goods and services soared. It is noteworthy that in 1977, the year before the Islamic revolution sharply reduced Iranian oil output, Saudi imports of goods and services exceeded those of Iran, whose population was five to six times as large. The large balance of payments (current account) surpluses of earlier years were steadily diminishing and by 1978 a deficit had emerged. The central bank of Saudi Arabia cautioned that without a substantial increase in oil revenues, or significant cutbacks in expenditures, deficits would persist, and would exhaust the financial reserves accumulated in earlier years.

The revolution in Iran, which sharply reduced its exports, came to the rescue—or so it appeared to the Saudis and others at the time. Iran under the Shah had become the world's second largest oil exporter, and the near cessation of exports triggered massive speculative buying, soaring oil prices, and an increased demand for Saudi oil. The Saudi government's oil revenues soared from $33-34 billion per annum in 1976-79 to over $96 billion in fiscal year 1980-81.[1] Oil analysts were almost unanimous in their view that prices which had risen from $11-12 per barrel in 1978 to almost $40 in 1981 would continue to rise and that the market would demand even more Saudi oil. Saudi Arabia, which alone possesses about one-fourth of world oil reserves, would by this analysis continue to enjoy the best of both worlds—a greater volume of exports and still higher prices. Senior American officials were sent to Riyadh to urge a further expansion of Saudi productive capacity in order to satisfy the anticipated growth in demand for Saudi oil.[2]

The trebling of oil revenues led to further acceleration in Saudi public spending, which more than doubled from 1977-78 to 1981-82, rising from $39 billion to $84 billion. The even more grandiose economic development plan for 1980-85, adopted in 1980, called for public expenditures of $390 billion, as compared with the $142 billion called for in the 1975-80 plan. It was based on the premise that Saudi oil revenues would continue to expand, as projected by almost all oil analysts at the time. The categories of planned spending were similar to those of the 1975-80 plan—only more so. Their plan called for increases in spending on infrastructure, the military forces and educational and health services; very generous subsidies to consumers and

---

[1] See Appendices—Tables 2-4.

[2] For details and sources see the present author's studies, "The Diminishing Importance of Middle Eastern Oil" in C. Legum, H. Shaked, and D. Dishon, eds., *Middle East Contemporary Survey*, Volume V, 1982; "Saudi Arabia's Dismal Economic Future" in *Middle East Contemporary Survey*, Volume IX, 1987; and "Middle East Oil Power: Mirage or Reality?" in H. Esfandiari and A.L. Udovich, eds., *The Economic Dimensions of Middle Eastern History*, Princeton, New Jersey: Darwin Press, 1990.

producers; a greater emphasis on the development of modern industry and agriculture; and increased foreign aid, largely to the neighboring Arab countries. There was a massive influx of millions of foreign workers from the poorer Arab and Asian states, as well as skilled and high-level managerial personnel from the advanced industrialized countries.

1982-89—THE RUDE AWAKENING

The events of 1982-83 came as a shocker, with a precipitous $42 billion decline in oil revenues, from $97 billion in 1981-82 to $54 billion in the following year. The Saudis appear to have initially accepted the view of oil analysts that this was a temporary digression from longer term trends, and largely attributable to the recession in the major industrialized countries and the consequent drop in oil demand. The Saudis began to curb expenditures, but far less than the drop in revenues, and the deterioration in Saudi finances was dramatic. In fiscal year 1980-81, there had been a record budgetary surplus of $34 billion, followed by a sizeable $25 billion surplus in 1981-82. In the following year the budget was in approximate balance, but from that point on there were **large deficits in every year since 1983.** Measured as a ratio of gross domestic product (GDP), the deficits were as a high as one-fourth of GDP in 1987 and in 1988, and one-sixth of GDP in 1989.[1]

The fiscal deterioration was inevitably followed by large deficits in the balance of payments (the current account). In every year since 1983, balance of payments deficits persisted, and **between 1983 and 1989 Saudi Arabia's cumulative current account deficits added up to a massive $85 billion.** As a result, central bank foreign assets dropped sharply from $138 billion at the end of 1982 to $63 billion at the end of 1988—a severe decline of $75 billion, according to the official accounts.[2] In actuality, central bank foreign assets were far lower in 1988 than the $63 billion figure since they included fictitious assets,

---

[1] See Appendices—Tables 3 and 4 and notes. Since 1987 the Saudi fiscal year has corresponded to the common calendar year, rather than the Muslim year.

[2] See Appendices—Table 2.

namely, loans extended to Iraq during its war with Iran (1980-88) as well as to some other poor Arab countries. While Iraqi authorities repeatedly stated that these were "contributions" to the "Arab" war against Iran and not loans, the Saudi central bank included them as assets. In the midst of the Kuwait crisis, the Saudi monarch revealed that his country's aid to Iraq in 1980-88 amounted to: $5.8 billion in cash grants; $9.2 billion in concessionary (long-term interest-free) loans; $6.8 billion in oil (to be repaid eventually by oil shipments from Iraq); and $3.7 billion in military equipment and other items.[1] Taking into account other fictitious assets held by the central bank, such as loans to Egypt and other Arab countries, its real foreign assets at the end of 1988 were no more than $40 billion, and probably less, a decline of close to $100 billion from the peak levels of mid-1982.

The authorities did take steps to reduce budgetary outlays and drew them down from a peak of $84 billion in fiscal year 1981-82 to $39 billion in 1989. The bulk of cutbacks were in the "projects" budget, i.e., investments in infrastructure, along with reductions in reported military expenditures—but these may have been offset, in part, by off-budgetary outlays such as the barter agreement with the British manufacturer of Tornado military aircraft in exchange for oil shipments. Foreign aid—as reported in the budget—was also cut sharply but this does not take into account the off-budgetary "loans" to Iraq noted above.

Yet, the regime hardly touched the wide range of subsidies, both to producers and consumers, and social welfare spending. In Saudi Arabia these policies include "creating" white collar government jobs, as the regime is especially concerned with the prospects of large numbers of unemployed university and secondary school graduates, who if idle and discontented, might endanger political and social stability. Hence many are "employed" by the civil service—further aggravating the budgetary deficits. Suggestions by the Ministry of Finance to curb some "entitlements," even mildly, have in the past been summarily rejected by the King,[2] who is apparently concerned that such measures might create discontent, especially since the extended royal family, and other

---

[1] *Middle East Economic Digest (MEED)*, January 25, 1991, p. 26.

[2] *Middle East Review 1989*, London, p. 132.

members of the elite, continue to live lavishly. In other words, given its political and social constraints, the regime felt that spending cutbacks had their limits.

The sharp drop in foreign assets and the continued deficits persuaded the authorities to seek loans to cover all or most of the deficits rather than risk a further depletion of foreign assets. For Saudi Arabia, state borrowing represented a radical departure from its long-time policies. In his presentation of the 1987 budget, the King stated that "the government has tried its best in these difficult circumstances to keep the welfare of its citizens in mind while not burdening itself with loans, either external or internal."[1] A year later the authorities announced the sale of government bonds. By the end of 1989 about $20 billion had been sold, of which some three-fourths were acquired by quasi-governmental agencies, and most of the balance by local commercial banks. In addition, the state-owned Public Investment Fund borrowed some $660 million in mid-1989 from Saudi and Gulf-based banks. Some state-owned companies (such as subsidiaries of the Saudi Basic Industries Corp.) borrowed from commercial banks, though previously they had had access to direct loans from the treasury. Moreover, as the decline in oil prices had to be offset by cash payments, in the mid-1980s the state borrowed from international banks to cover payments to British Aerospace for the purchase of Tornado military aircraft, spending which is outside the published budget.[2] The state's financial stringency also expressed itself in delayed payments to contractors, foreign as well as domestic. The U.S. Embassy in Riyadh noted in its report for 1989 that "payment delays are sometimes used by the government to extract additional services (not called for in the contract) . . . and firms are frequently asked to settle for less in order to be paid."[3]

In short, the Saudi state's financial situation—by which is meant the state treasury, and not the private wealth of the

---

[1] Cited in The National Bank of Kuwait, *Kuwait and Gulf Cooperation Council—Economic and Financial Bulletin*, Fall 1987, p. 24.

[2] *Middle East Economic Survey (MEES)*, February 18, 1991, pp. B1 and B2.

[3] U.S. Department of Commerce, *Foreign Economic Trends-Saudi Arabia* October 1989, pp. 6 7.

monarch, the thousands of princes, and some other very wealthy Saudis—was precarious during the latter half of the 1980s.

CHANGES IN SAUDI OIL POLICIES BEFORE THE GULF CRISIS

By the mid-1980s the Saudi authorities had come to the realization that the decline in oil prices since 1981 was not a temporary digression, but rather a longer term reaction of energy markets to the high prices of the early 1980s. Moreover, even the sharp drop in Iraqi and Iranian exports as a consequence of the Iran-Iraq war did not suffice to sustain oil prices.

The years since 1985 have seen a sharp change in Saudi oil policies. In 1982, OPEC decided, for the first time, to allocate maximum production quotas designed to curb output in order to bolster sagging oil prices. Saudi Arabia assumed the role of "swing" producer, i.e., it would undertake to balance supply and demand for OPEC oil. But as demand dropped far more than anticipated, and a number of OPEC members were "cheating" on their quotas—producing more than the cartel had sanctioned—Saudi sales and revenues dropped precipitously. Saudi production, which had been close to 10 MBD in 1979-81, dropped to 3.2 MBD in 1985. Oil export revenues fell from a peak of $111 billion in 1981 to $24 billion in 1985 and $17 billion in the following year.

The cause for this was that high oil prices had boomeranged, reducing world demand for oil generally, and for OPEC oil, in particular. The 1973 oil shock initiated a trend towards improved energy efficiency, and within the "basket" of energy sources, a trend towards fuel-switching away from oil. Moreover, high oil prices provided stronger incentives for oil and gas exploration world-wide. The strong growth in oil production world-wide further weakened the demand for OPEC oil. The much higher oil prices of the 1979-80 oil shock gave an additional and more powerful boost to improvements in energy efficiency, and increased substitution of other sources of energy for oil. Thus the demand for oil fell, but for OPEC the decline was steeper, and within OPEC the Saudis bore the brunt of the decline. Since the mid-1980s they have concluded that their most vital national interests dictate a policy of moderate oil prices, and a greater volume of production and exports—not higher prices.

THE KUWAIT CRISIS AND SAUDI FINANCES

Following the Iraqi invasion of Kuwait, the United Nations imposed sanctions on oil shipments from Iraq and occupied Kuwait. In the September-December quarter, Iraqi production dropped sharply from 3.1 MBD during the first half of 1990 to 500 TBD (thousands of barrels per day) while Kuwait's output dropped from 1.9 MBD to 100 TBD.[1] Insofar as international trade is concerned (excluding domestic consumption of Iraq and Kuwait) there was a cutback of 4.4 MBD. Oil markets reacted by raising prices to much higher levels, in part out of the fear that hostilities might spread to Saudi Arabia, the United Arab Emirates and Qatar, and destroy oil installations in those countries.

Saudi Arabia invited the U.S.-led coalition to deploy its forces in the country and undertook to pay, in part, for the costs of the military forces sent by the U.S., the UK, Egypt, Syria and others in the anti-Iraq coalition. It also undertook to make payments to Turkey and others which suffered, indirectly, from their adherence to the UN sanctions imposed on Iraq. The precise magnitude of Saudi commitments has not been revealed officially, but independent estimates range between $45 billion and $60 billion.[2] To put these figures into perspective, it might be noted that Saudi oil export revenues in 1988 and 1989 *combined* were $44 billion.[3] In light of Saudi Arabia's financial problems during the latter half of the 1980s, and its fear of a repetition of the boom and bust cycle of the 1980s, the Saudi authorities decided to step up oil production both in order to maximize revenues and to restrain the sharp increases in oil prices. Saudi output rose from 5.6 MBD in the first half of 1990 to an average of 8.2 MBD in September-

---

[1] Unless otherwise stated all figures for oil production are from *Petroleum Economist*, monthly, London. See Appendices—Table 1.

[2] This includes $19.6 billion pledged to the U.S. The overall estimates include incremental military outlays on the part of Saudi Arabia. *MEED*, May 24, 1991, pp. 4, 5, 26.

[3] See Appendices—Table 4.

December 1990. In the latter month output reached a 1990 peak of 8.6 MBD. Increased Saudi output compensated for over half of the reduction in Iraqi and Kuwaiti output, while most of the balance was made up by Venezuela, Abu Dhabi, Libya, Nigeria, Indonesia, Norway and others.

Production of 8-8.5 MBD proved to be beyond Saudi Arabia's sustainable capacity, with the result that the fields were being overworked and that a continuation of this rate of production threatened to damage "subterranean oil-field pressure and hence the [fields'] long term productive capacity."[1] Accordingly, in January 1991, the Saudis began to reduce output, which fell to 7.5 MBD by May.[2] In order to minimize the possible effects of future disruptions on oil production the Saudis are planning a large number of underground oil storage facilities in various parts of the country, at an estimated cost of $6 billion.[3] They are also proceeding with plans to expand the capacity of the East-West pipeline (Petroline) from 3.6 to 4.8 MBD. This pipeline would enable oil shipments to circumvent the Straits of Hormuz, in case of regional instability. At the same time, Saudi Aramco, the state-owned oil company, announced a sharp increase in drilling.[4] All of these actions are consistent with Saudi oil policy, which aims to acquire a greater share of the oil market and to keep prices in

---

[1] *MidEast Markets,* June 10, 1991, p. 4; *MEED,* June 7, 1991, p. 4.

[2] In 1989, the Saudi Oil Minister had announced that *sustained* production capacity would be raised to 10 MBD by 1996, at a cost of $30 billion. *The Economist Intelligence Unit (EIU): Country Report-Saudi Arabia,* No. 4, 1989, p. 16.

In June 1991 he announced an acceleration of the planned expansion to be completed by the end of 1994. Moreover, he stated categorically that production would be maintained at the current 8-8.5 MBD and would not return to the pre-crisis level of 5.4 MBD. *Wall Street Journal,* June 6, 1991, p. 4.

This statement was aimed at his colleagues in OPEC who will probably request that once Kuwait and Iraq re-enter the market, the Saudis should make room by implementing a significant reduction in their output.

[3] *MEED,* July 19, 1991, p. 26.

[4] *EIU: Country Report-Saudi Arabia,* No. 2, 1991, pp. 17-18.

check. The Saudis are not making these large investments in order to build up idle capacity. They simply cannot afford to.

At this writing (spring 1992) the Saudis have not published detailed reports with respect to actual budgetary revenues and outlays in 1991. Saudi officials report the actual budgetary deficit was $14.9 billion for 1990. Total revenues were $41.3 billion of which $31.5 billion came from oil. 1991 estimates by the IMF place expenditures at $75.3 billion and the deficit at $20.5 billion, which implies that the total revenues in 1991 were $54.8 billion. The planned budgetary deficit for 1992 is $8 billion.[1] Oil revenues in 1990 were about $8 billion above original projections; the higher prices and greater volume of exports in August-December 1990 had more than offset the decline in oil revenues in the first half of the year when prices were falling sharply. However, expenditures climbed far more rapidly and the deficit was greatly in excess of original projections.[2]

It is particularly noteworthy that even during wartime the regime took no measures to reduce the deficit either by imposing taxes, by curbing outlays on subsidies and a wide range of social welfare schemes, or by cutting back on the bloated state bureaucracy. Due to the exigencies and uncertainties arising from the war, no detailed budget was announced for 1991. However, what is again noteworthy are the budgetary directives, which stated that in the following areas spending would be maintained: salaries and allowances for state employees; large subsidies for agricultural production; subsidies for consumers, including food, electricity and other public utilities; social welfare payments; state lending for real estate, agriculture, and industry (at zero or nominal rates of interest); and outlays for various infrastructural projects and for their operations and maintenance.[3] In short, the Saudi welfare state would be maintained, war or no war.[4]

---

[1] *Financial Times*, February 18, 1992, p. 17.

[2] *Financial Times*, February 15, 1991, p. 3.

[3] *MEED*, January 18, 1991, p. 18.

[4] *Business Week*, February 25, 1991, p. 35.

In addition to standard welfare state expenditures, the large expansion in university education has created a rather new problem, namely, providing "suitable" employment for university graduates. In 1989, the U.S. Embassy in Riyadh reported that unemployment and underemployment were emerging as serious problems. Saudi university and high school graduates, basing their expectations on the boom years and not on present realities, expect well-paying white collar jobs in the bureaucracy.[1] In his presentation of the budget for 1990, the King stated that the armed forces would recruit 26,000 and would also provide 20,000 additional government jobs. This policy of make-work jobs in the bureaucracy may ameliorate internal social and political problems, but it can only aggravate the budgetary deficits of recent years.[2]

1991 was a year of large deficits. While the current account deficit was $4 billion in 1990, unofficial estimates are that this rose sharply to $24 billion in 1991. The deficit was equivalent to about 23 percent of the GDP.[3] The commitments undertaken by Saudi Arabia in relation to the crisis (i.e., payments to the U.S. and others who had stationed forces in Saudi Arabia, and to those to be compensated for losses related to the war) needed to be paid, for the most part, in 1990 and 1991. The official estimates for total war costs in 1990 and 1991 were $49.6 billion, of which the U.S. received $12.8 billion in cash plus $4 billion in kind.[4] The question is: what about the longer-term impact of the crisis?

THE LONGER-TERM ECONOMIC EFFECTS OF THE GULF CRISIS ON SAUDI ARABIA

Since the end of hostilities in February 1991, the Saudi authorities have announced plans for a major increase in their armed forces as well as a further upgrading and modernization of military equipment. The King stated that

---

[1] U.S. Department of Commerce, *Foreign Economic Trends-Saudi Arabia,* October 1989, pp. 6-7.

[2] *EIU: Country Report-Saudi Arabia,* No. 1, 1990, p. 9.

[3] *MEED*, March 20, 1992, p. 12.

[4] *MEED*, April 17, 1992, p. 22 and May 15, 1992, p. 6.

there was a "firm decision on the need for immediate action to expand and re-equip all sectors of our armed forces—ground, naval and air forces—with the world's most powerful and modern equipment and technology."[1] Prince Khaled Ibn Sultan, who commanded the Arab and Islamic forces arrayed against Iraq, asserted that there was no need to station U.S. or any other foreign forces permanently in his country, and instead urged tripling the size of the armed forces and enlarging and enhancing its weapons arsenal.[2] In line with these policies, Saudi Arabia has requested and received almost $7 billion in arms from the U.S. since the end of the Persian Gulf War. The Saudis are also waiting for approval on a $5 billion sale of F-15s. In addition to purchases from the U.S., the Saudis have concluded agreements with European countries including one with the French in December 1990 for anti-aircraft missiles. Two longer-term agreements had been concluded with the UK in 1985 and in 1988, for the supply of Tornado aircraft at a total cost of $30 billion.[3] There is no indication that these orders have been curtailed following the large request for additional American arms.

In 1984-85 (inclusive) Saudi arms purchases abroad totaled $19.5 billion, of which the main suppliers were: France, $7.5 billion; the U.S. $5.8 billion; China $2.5 billion and the UK $2.1 billion.[4] (These figures do not include payments to foreign contractors for the construction of military bases, training, maintenance, etc.) The decision to implement a major expansion of the armed forces and to acquire larger quantities of sophisticated military equipment implies **a quantum leap in Saudi military outlays for many years**. In 1986-89, (announced) military budgets averaged $13-14 billion per annum, as compared with $18-19 billion per annum in 1981-85.[5] Off-budgetary military outlays may well account for part of the

---

[1] *MEED*, April 26, 1991, p. 30.

[2] *The New York Times*, April 29, 1991, p. A10.

[3] *MEED*, December 7, 1990, p. 16.

[4] U.S. Arms Control and Disarmament Agency, *World Military Expenditures and Arms Transfers* 1989, p. 118.

[5] See Saudi Arabia—Table 4.

decline in the announced budgets in the latter half of the 1980s. But it seems plausible that there was some reduction in military outlays in the latter half of the 1980s in light of financial constraints. As for the future, it appears reasonably certain that Saudi military spending will be greatly expanded. This, in turn, has important implications for Saudi Arabia's financial situation, and, indirectly, for its oil policies.

Since significant reductions in civilian expenditures and/or new taxes are apparently not politically feasible, Riyadh has decided to seek large loans from international as well as local and regional banks. In May 1991, a consortium of twenty international banks signed an agreement with Saudi Arabia for a loan of $4.5 billion. In addition the government borrowed $2.5 billion from local banks. They were given no choice in the matter and each was assigned a minimum "contribution." These figures do not include loans made to public and semi-public companies.[1] Between 1983 and 1988, the government financed its deficits by drawing down its financial reserves accumulated in the "years of plenty." Since 1988, and especially since the Kuwait crisis, the government has had increasing recourse to debt, external and domestic, to finance its deficits.

For the long term, increased Saudi borrowing implies that future budgets will have to provide substantial funds for servicing the growing public debt (payments of principal and interest). The contrast with earlier years is marked. In fiscal year 1982-83 and again in 1983-84, investment income received by the government from foreign assets was as high as $14 billion per annum. This source of revenue dwindled during the 1980s to less than $3 billion in 1989 and only $208 million by the end of the third period of 1990.[2] This was due both to the decline in Saudi foreign assets as well as lower interest rates abroad. Servicing the growing public debt will surely aggravate budgetary deficits.

A final element of Saudi fiscal policy arises from its relationship to the poorer Arab nations. During the course of the 1980s, Saudi financial aid to the poorer Arab countries was sharply reduced. According to the announced budgets (which,

---

[1] *Financial Times*, May 14, 1991, p. 4; *MEED*, June 21, 1991, pp. 20-21.

[2] See Appendices—Table 2.

apparently, do not include aid to Iraq during the war with Iran) foreign aid dropped from a peak of over $7 billion per annum in the early 1980s to less than $2 billion per annum in 1988 and 1989.[1]

What about the future? Saddam Hussein did all he could to exploit the wide gap between living standards in the rich Arab oil states and the poverty afflicting tens of millions of Arabs in the poor countries. Indeed, there were popular demonstrations in these countries in support of Saddam Hussein. As one observer noted: "The harsh truth [is] that Kuwait, Saudi Arabia, and other big oil producers in the Gulf region have found a deep current of Arab dislike for them."[2] The sharp cutback in Saudi aid in the 1980s (and similar measures by Kuwait and other oil-rich states) aggravated the recession in the poor Arab countries during the second half of the 1980s. In the future Saudi Arabia will be far more cautious in this regard. While it is unlikely that it will return to the relatively generous levels of aid of the early 1980s, the aftermath of the Kuwait crisis probably implies higher levels of aid than might otherwise have been granted. The Kuwait crisis has heightened the importance the Saudi leadership attaches to foreign aid. It is, as it were, an element of the country's defense budget.

IMPLICATIONS FOR SAUDI OIL POLICIES

In January 1991, the Saudi ambassador to the U.S., responding to accusations that his country had been enriched by the higher oil revenues arising from the crisis, asserted that "higher oil prices since early August are expected by practically all international energy experts to decline after the crisis. But expenditures resulting from the crisis and its aftermath are anticipated to be *significant and long lasting*" (emphasis added).[3] The short-term expenditures were mainly payments to the U.S. and others who joined the coalition against Iraq, as well as increased Saudi military expenditures during the crisis and hostilities. As for the long term, the

---

[1] See Appendices—Table 2.

[2] *The New York Times,* August 12, 1990, p. E2.

[3] *MEED,* January 18, 1991, p. 18.

aftermath of the crisis has seen a major build-up of the armed forces, a political need to increase aid to the poorer Arab countries, and a growing burden of foreign debt.

Internal political constraints severely restrict the ability of the authorities to reduce civilian expenditures and/or to increase revenues by imposing taxes. In short, the authorities must seek ways to increase oil revenues. **With the memories of the 1980s still fresh, the Saudis are strongly opposed to any significant increase in oil prices. This leaves the Saudis with one alternative: increase the volume of production and exports.** Six months after the war, *The Economist* noted: "Oil price has been lower than most analysts predicted. King Fahd is concerned about his country's long-term share of the oil-market, and oil's place among fuels (high oil prices induce more fuel-switching). Both are helped by a low price. Since the Gulf War the Saudis, no longer inhibited by Iraq, have been able to pursue these policies more openly. A policy of moderately-priced oil has become more pressing. Carbon and gasoline taxes (imposed in a number of major oil-consuming countries) threaten some oil markets; liquefied natural gas (substituting for oil) threatens others."[1]

There is little doubt that fear of Iraq inhibited Saudi oil production before the Kuwait crisis. This was especially true following the mid-1988 cease-fire that ended the war between Iraq and Iran. In July 1990, a few weeks before the invasion of Kuwait, Saddam Hussein issued threats against Kuwait and the United Arab Emirates, the major "violators" of OPEC quotas. Surely they were also aimed at Saudi Arabia, and other "overproducers."[2] During the first half of 1990 UAE overproduction was 735 TBD; Kuwait's, 430 TBD; and Saudi Arabia's, 235 TBD; The U.S. commitment to defend Saudi Arabia allayed Saudi fears and production rose sharply from 5.6 MBD in the first half of 1990 to 7.9 MBD in the first half of 1991. Looking to the future, the Saudis have announced an acceleration of their plans to expand production capacity. With American protection Saudi oil policies are no longer affected

---

[1] *The Economist,* August 11, 1991, p. 41.

[2] *San Francisco Chronicle-Associated Press,* July 19, 1990, p. A13.

by fear of Iraq. This enhances the likelihood that **Saudi oil production will be expanded further during the coming years.**[1]

---

[1] It is interesting to note a prediction made in June 1991 by a former Saudi Deputy Minister of Finance: "If Saudi Arabia continues to require a high level of oil income to finance a growing budget and current account (balance of payments) deficit, the only way to do this is by dumping the market with more oil supplies. . . Prices can only go downward." *MEED*, July 19, 1991, pp. 4-5. Another former minister, Sheikh Yamani, expressed similar views stating (in early 1991) that Saudi Arabia's financial requirements would make it difficult to restrain production. He expressed his belief that Saudi Arabia would raise capacity beyond the announced goal of 10 MBD, to 13 MBD. *MEED*, February 1, 1991, p. 5; *Oil and Gas Journal*, February 25, 1991. Presumably this would take place during the 1990s.

II KUWAIT

Saudi Arabia is by no means alone in its drive to increase oil revenues by expanding production capacity and exports. This policy antedates the Gulf War, but the war intensified the drive, especially in those countries most affected by it. As *The New York Times* noted: "All members of OPEC have reached the conclusion that if it is to survive it must treat oil as a commodity, not a political weapon. Yesterday's price hawks, including Algeria, Iran and Libya [now advocate] moderate prices."[1]

KUWAIT BEFORE THE INVASION

While Saudi Arabia and other major Middle Eastern oil-exporting countries encountered large deficits since 1983 and as a result drew down their financial reserves, Kuwait was very much the exception. Although lower oil prices did reduce Kuwait's (commodity) export revenues (overwhelmingly from oil) from a peak of $20.6 billion in 1980 to $11.4 billion in 1989, its large and growing investments abroad continued to yield handsome dividends and interest. The export of services (in the case of Kuwait, largely investment income from abroad) reached an all-time peak in 1989 of $10.2 billion, not far below oil export revenues in that year. The balance on current account (i.e., exports of goods and services minus imports of goods and services and grants to foreign countries) after declining from a peak of $15.3 billion in 1980 to about $4.5

---

[1] *The New York Times*, December 16, 1990, p. F12.

billion in 1987, rose to $8.4 billion in 1989. In other words Kuwaiti foreign assets continued to rise in the period 1982-89, though at a lesser rate than before. This was in sharp contrast to Saudi Arabia and other oil-exporting countries which were depleting their financial reserves and were accumulating debt.[1]

Before the Iraqi invasion, the population of Kuwait was estimated at 1.6 million, with citizens accounting for less than 40 percent. With respect to the labor force, Kuwaitis accounted for an even smaller fraction—under one-fifth. Like Saudi Arabia, Kuwait developed and financed a vast welfare system for its citizens, including free health and educational services, up to and including university education at the highest levels. It went so far as to guarantee its citizens housing with maid's quarters, and maids were duly imported from poor Asian countries.[2]

Why then did Saudi Arabia encounter growing financial problems while Kuwait steadily amassed financial reserves during the 1980s? This is partly because Saudi Arabia spent vast sums on the development of modern industry and, to a lesser extent, agriculture. These were based largely on imported labor (skilled and unskilled), foreign managers, and heavy subsidies. Kuwait, by contrast, invested far less in the development of local industry, laying great emphasis on the acquisition of industrial and other assets in the developed Western countries, which would yield a growing stream of investment income. In this, the Kuwaitis were eminently successful. They also spent far less on their armed forces, presumably on the assumption that there was little they could do to resist aggression on the part of Iraq or Iran. Between 1983 and 1988, Kuwait's military budget was less than $1.5 billion per annum, or 5-6 percent of GNP. During the same period the Saudis spent $19 billion per annum on defense, or 20 percent of GNP.[3] Official figures also show that grants to the poor Arab

------

[1] This is based on the monthly International Monetary Fund *International Financial Statistics.*

[2] *The New York Times*, August 8, 1991, p. A11.

[3] U.S. Arms Control and Disarmament Agency *World Military Expenditures and Arms Transfers*, 1989, pp. 54, 63.

states were reduced from a peak of almost $1 billion in 1981 to less than $200 million per annum in 1986-89. Meanwhile, Kuwait also extended off-budgetary "loans" to Iraq similar to those made by Saudi Arabia and the UAE, which were, as *The Financial Times*, put it, a form of "danegeld" ("protection money" in the American slang).[1] Kuwait's geographic location made it particularly susceptible to Iraqi "requests" for additional cash. One estimate is that Kuwaiti aid to Iraq from 1980-88 was at least $13.5 billion. Shortly after the invasion of his country, Kuwait's ruler claimed that Iraq's war debt to Kuwait was $14-15 billion.[2]

While Kuwait was *relatively* prudent in its public expenditures, it was also far more aggressive in augmenting its revenues (its policies with respect to foreign investment are noted above). It also tended to ignore OPEC quotas which might have reduced, or reduced further, its oil export revenues. In 1987-89, Kuwait's quota was about 1.0 MBD; its actual production was 1.4 MBD in 1987-88, rising to 1.8 MBD in 1989. In 1990, its quota was raised to 1.5 MBD; actual production averaged 1.9 MBD in the first half of 1990. While Saudi Arabia and others also exceeded their quotas, Kuwait's "over-production" was the greatest, with the exception of the UAE. In February 1990, the Kuwaiti Oil Minister stated publicly that he had given orders to produce 2 MBD, while his country's quota was 1.5 MBD. At the same time, Kuwait was expanding its marketing commitments for the supply of crude oil to the refineries abroad which it owned fully or in partnership with foreign oil companies.[3] In a press interview given towards the end of 1989, Kuwait's Oil Minister asserted that he wanted oil prices to remain at the $18 level "for at least three or four years."[4] This implied a steady erosion in oil prices, measured in real (inflation-corrected) dollars. With its enormous oil reserves—over 90 billion barrels—Kuwait was concerned with the long-term future of oil

---

[1] *Financial Times*, August 7, 1990, p. 2; International Monetary Fund *International Financial Statistics*, various issues.

[2] *Financial Times*, August 18-19, 1990, p. 3.

[3] *Financial Times*, February 22, 1990, p. 34.

[4] *Middle East Economic Survey*, December 4, 1989, p. D6.

markets, which would be adversely affected by higher prices. In any case, as a result of its policies, Kuwaiti oil revenues fell far less, proportionately, than those of Saudi Arabia. In 1989 Saudi oil export revenues were about one-fifth their peak levels of the early 1980s; Kuwait's were only down by about half. Moreover, as noted earlier, Kuwait's investment income was at an all-time high in 1989; Saudi Arabia's had declined sharply.

Kuwait's official financial reserves were, and are, a state secret; unofficial estimates vary. The cumulative current account balances between 1975-89 add up to over $110 billion.[1] However, the $110 billion figure includes privately-owned foreign assets (including those of the ruler and the royal family, as well as those of other wealthy Kuwaitis), and fictitious assets, i.e., loans made to Iraq, Egypt, Syria and other poor Arab states, whose prospects of repayment are effectively nil.

The figure for official Kuwaiti foreign assets most widely quoted in mid-1990 was about $100 billion.[2] Another estimate suggested that state investments abroad—excluding loans to Arab countries—were about $80 billion. In addition some $25-30 billion were held abroad by individuals and corporations.[3] Still another estimate suggested that Kuwait's financial reserves in mid-1988 were $90 billion, of which $60 billion was held by the Reserve Fund for Future Generations, almost all of which is invested in the West, and another $30 billion by the (other) State Reserve Fund, most of which is "invested" in loans to Arab countries and to the many Kuwaitis affected by the "stock market" crash in 1982.[4] In other words, real state-held foreign assets were not much above $60 billion in mid-1988. One can assume that they rose by possibly another $10-15 billion by mid-1990.

---

[1] Balance of payments estimates for earlier years are unavailable. In any case, they would modify the picture only at the margins. See International Monetary Fund *International Financial Statistics Yearbook*, 1990, p. 463.

[2] *The New York Times*, August 7, 1990, pp. 1, A8.

[3] *The New York Times*, August 13, 1990, p. D3.

[4] *The Economist*, August 4, 1990, pp. 51-52.

KUWAIT'S ECONOMY SINCE THE INVASION

The destruction wrought by the hostilities of 1990-91 and the massive Iraqi looting and sabotage—especially the torching of most oil wells before Iraq's withdrawal—mandate extensive and expensive reconstruction. Initial estimates have been scaled down considerably, but even the lower estimates indicate that the costs of repair and reconstruction, plus financial compensation to the U.S. and other allies, will constitute a major drain on Kuwait's foreign assets for a number of years. The announced plans also include compensation and special allocations to Kuwaiti citizens and businesses. In other words, the policy of generous handouts by the Kuwaiti welfare state will continue.

It will be a number of years before Kuwait's oil output is restored to prewar levels, and the concomitant loss of oil revenues will further complicate Kuwait's financial problems. The war cost Kuwait $65 billion, which deeply cut into its assets of nearly $100 billion.[1] Also the budget for 1992 incorporated a $17 billion deficit that needs to be financed by borrowing.[2] In mid-1991 it was reported that Kuwait had already liquidated about $15 billion of its overseas assets.[3] In order to conserve these assets it has decided to seek large loans abroad—possibly up to $20 billion over the next few years.[4] A UN team assigned to assess war damages estimated reconstruction costs at about $20 billion, not including "unquantified damage to . . . education and health, water supply and garbage disposal systems and agriculture and fisheries. Hidden losses include the damage to the country's oil reservoirs as a result of uncontrolled gushing from sabotaged wells."[5] Unofficial projections for 1991 see a current

---

[1] *The New York Times*, April 20, 1992, p. A2.

[2] *Ibid.*

[3] *Wall Street Journal*, July 8, 1991, p. 1.

[4] *Financial Times Survey-Rebuilding Kuwait*, July 8, 1991, p. iv.

[5] *Ibid*, p. vi.

account *deficit* of $22.5 billion,[1] a sharp contrast to the unbroken series of current account surpluses of the 1970s and 1980s.

In mid-1991 the Kuwaitis stated that the restoration of oil production was proceeding and that by the end of the year production should reach 400 TBD.[2] Production is reported to have reached 1.0 MBD in April 1992 (with domestic consumption around 100 TBD) and is expected to rise to 1.5 MBD by the end of 1992.[3] There is little doubt that over the next few years Kuwait will restore its prewar production and then exceed it. Despite the sabotaging of its oil wells, its reserves are enormous. The Oil Minister stated (September 1991) that the *permanent* damage to the country's oil reserves of 100 billion barrels was perhaps roughly 3 percent. The remaining reserves are almost three times those of the U.S.[4]

In the aftermath of the war, the motivation to maximize production—regardless of OPEC decisions—will be even stronger than in the past. In November 1990—before the large-scale and wanton sabotage of his country by the retreating Iraqi army—the Kuwaiti Oil Minister told his colleagues in OPEC that after liberation his country would "need huge amounts of revenue to rebuild Kuwait."[5] If fear of Iraq or Iran might have deterred Kuwait in the past from fully utilizing its oil production capacity, the Persian Gulf War, and the recently-concluded defense agreements with the U.S. and other Western countries, should remove future hesitations.[6] Kuwait has joined Saudi Arabia and other oil exporters who are incurring deficits and are in need of more oil revenues—now.

---

[1] *MEED*, July 19, 1991, pp. 4-5.

[2] *Petroleum Intelligence Weekly*, July 10, 1991, p. 3.

[3] *Wall Street Journal*, April 27, 1992, p. A2.

[4] *MEED*, October 4, 1991, p. 30.

[5] *MEED*, November 2, 1990, p. 15.

[6] *MEED*, September 27, 1991, p. 22.

III IRAQ

Iraq's oil reserves of 100 billion barrels are second only to those of Saudi Arabia. Unlike the neighboring Gulf states, it also possesses abundant cultivable land and water, as well as various minerals. From the point of view of natural resources it is richly endowed. But the war with Iran in the 1980s and the more recent Persian Gulf War and its aftermath have brought ruination to its economy, from which it will take many years, possibly a decade or longer, to recover.

THE ECONOMIC IMPACT OF THE WAR WITH IRAN

Iraqi oil production, which stood at 1.5 MBD in 1969, expanded to 3.5 MBD in 1979 and oil export revenues escalated from $0.8 billion in 1969 to $21.4 billion in 1979, mainly as a consequence of much higher prices. In the first eight months of 1980 (before the war with Iran) oil revenues were being generated at a rate of well over $30 billion per annum.[1] While oil revenues fueled large-scale spending on economic development, the adoption of socialist policies since the 1960s hampered the growth of the non-oil sectors. Agricultural production in 1979-81 (three-year average) was no higher than a decade earlier; on a per capita basis the decline was almost 30 percent. The agricultural trade deficit (farm exports minus farm imports) rose from less than $100 million per annum in

---

[1] *BP Statistical Review of World Energy,* June 1991, and earlier issues; *Middle East Economic Survey,* November 19, 1990.

1969-71 to over $800 million per annum in 1979-81.[1] Iraq had once been called the breadbasket of the Near East, but adverse economic policies made the country increasingly dependent on food imports.

Beginning in the mid-1970s, there was a very sharp escalation in military expenditures, as arms imports rose from an annual level of $0.6 billion in 1973-75 to $3.2 billion in 1979.[2] In retrospect, the military build-up paved the way to the attack on Iran in 1980, from which Saddam Hussein apparently expected a quick victory. Instead, the bloody eight-year war set back Iraq's economy for many years.

In addition to the hundreds of thousands of killed and wounded, some sectors of the civilian economy suffered serious direct physical damage. The port city of Basra and its environs were especially hard hit. Though Iraq's air superiority protected its oil installations from serious damage, Iran successfully blockaded Iraqi oil and other shipments through the Persian Gulf. It also formed an alliance with Syria persuading Damascus to close the pipeline from northern Iraq through its territory in return for generous compensation. This left Iraq with one small export outlet—the pipeline through Turkey. This volume of Iraqi oil exports dropped sharply from 3.2 MBD before the war to about 0.7 MBD in 1983, and as prices began to decline after 1981, oil revenues were reduced to about $10 billion in 1983, about a quarter of their 1979 level.

Despite the imposition of a strict austerity regime and a sharp reduction in civilian imports, the (civilian) trade surplus, which had been as high as $35 billion in 1979, was followed by large deficits. In addition, arms imports, not included in the trade figures, took on gargantuan dimensions, rising from $3.2 billion in 1979 to $9.2 billion in 1984. **Iraq had become the world's chief arms importer.**[3] The balance of payments deficits (the current account) were initially financed by drawing

---

[1] U.S. Department of Agriculture, various publications.

[2] U.S. Arms Control Disarmament Agency *World Military Expenditures and Arms Transfers*, 1989, and earlier issues.

[3] The figures for exports and imports are from IMF, *International Financial Statistics*, various issues; estimates of arms imports are from the above-mentioned publications of the U.S. Arms Control and Disarmament Agency.

down the $35 billion in foreign exchange reserves with which it entered the wars, and by generous aid from the rich Arab states. But as the war dragged on and large deficits persisted, Iraq sought and received credits from its foreign suppliers of civilian and military goods. The suppliers were quite a diverse group, and included many European countries, the U.S., the USSR, India, Turkey and others. Severe manpower shortages were offset, in part, by the importation of foreign labor from Egypt and from the poor Arab states. While no official figures are available, unofficial estimates range between one and two million expatriate workers, mainly Egyptians. But the remittances sent home by the foreigners (i.e., the import of services) also required the allocation of scarce foreign exchange. The austerity regime designed to restrict imports had a very adverse effect on living standards. The shortage of imported machinery, spare parts, and raw materials severely hampered the productive sectors of the economy.

By 1982 or so, the Iraqi authorities came to the realization that the war with Iran would be protracted, and they began to seek alternative routes for oil exports. They expanded the pipeline through Turkey and also laid down a new pipeline through Saudi Arabia. Much smaller quantities were trucked through Jordan. Exports rose from a low of 740 TBD in 1983 to 2.2 MBD in 1988, the year hostilities came to an end. However, since oil prices were dropping, oil export revenues rose far more modestly, from $7.8 billion in 1983 to $11.4 billion in 1987 and $11 billion in 1988. Most of the decline in prices in 1988 was offset by a higher volume of exports.[1] 1987-88 oil revenues were significantly higher than in 1983-86, but were still only one-half of oil export earnings in 1979, even when measured in current dollars, and far less in real dollars. Moreover, in the interim Iraq was saddled with the enormous costs of prosecuting the war, the pressing needs of repairing war damages, payments due on the huge debts accumulated during the war, as well as financing the importation of the most essential goods, especially food. Whenever payments came due the Iraqis would press lenders to "reschedule" all or part of the debt. More often than not the lenders agreed, both because they had little alternative and because they hoped that when hostilities eventually ended, Iraq, with its huge oil

---

[1] *Middle East Economic Survey,* November 20, 1990.

potential, would have no problem repaying the loans. Moreover, foreign lenders believed that post-war Iraq, with its huge needs for reconstruction and development, would prove to be a major market for their goods and services.

BETWEEN THE WARS—1988-1990

Hostilities with Iran ended in mid-1988 and Baghdad announced ambitious plans for reconstruction and economic development. The size of Iraq's foreign debt, and the magnitude of its debt service (annual payments on account of principal and interest) are state secrets. While one media report suggested that the foreign debt was "between $50 and $150 billion," the U.S. Embassy in Baghdad estimated that the "hard debt" (i.e., excluding so-called loans from Saudi Arabia and Kuwait) was $50 billion. Moreover, the report noted that, even after the cease-fire, arms imports continued at $5 billion annually.[1]

By the spring of 1990 Iraqi production had risen to 3.2 MBD (very close to its peak in 1979-80) and the oil ministry announced that its goal was to expand capacity by another 2 MBD by 1995.[2] However, due to lack of foreign exchange, the government said it would seek forcing companies to finance the expansion in return for future oil shipments from the newly-developed fields.[3]

Yet the plans for reconstruction and development were severely hampered by the lack of foreign exchange. Aside from some small loans, aid from Saudi Arabia and Kuwait had ceased. The U.S. Embassy estimated inflation at "no less than 40 percent."[4] Official figures confirmed a sharp decline in investment and living standards.[5] Higher oil prices and a larger volume of exports raised oil revenues in 1989 to $14.5

---

[1] U.S. Department of Commerce, *Foreign Economic Trends—Iraq*, September 1989, p. 4.

[2] *MEED*, March 2, 1990, p. 18.

[3] *The Middle East*, London (monthly), May 1990, pp. 29-30.

[4] *Ibid*, p. 4.

[5] *EIU: Country Report—Iraq*, No. 3, 1990, p. 13.

billion, as compared with $11 billion in the previous year.[1] But debt servicing requirements for 1990 had risen to about $8 billion ($5 billion on account of principal and $3 billion on account of interest).[2] Saddam Hussein had promised his people a "fat peace dividend" after their sacrifices and years of deprivation during eight years of war with Iran.[3] Two years had passed since the cease-fire and there was little evidence of economic betterment. On the contrary, inflation was rampant, even higher than during the war, and living standards for the large majority of the population were continuing to fall. Not only did the foreign debt fail to decline after the war, it rose by another $10 billion in the two years following the cease-fire with Iran.[4]

The drop in investment meant that the prospects for future economic growth were poor. The financial squeeze was worsening, as foreign lenders were becoming increasingly reluctant to extend further credits to finance work on the development of petrochemicals, oil, fertilizers, power stations and other projects. The U.S., which had been extending credits of about $1 billion per year for food purchases, announced that, for 1990, these credits would be cut back to $500 million.[5] This meant that Iraq had to use more of its scarce foreign currency to import essential food supplies.[6] By this time, Iraq was dependent on imports for 70 percent of its food supplies.[7]

During the first half of 1990 the economy was continuing to deteriorate while the prospects for improvement in the near future became even more remote. In the first six months of

---

[1] *Middle East Economic Survey*, November 19, 1990.

[2] *EIU: Country Report—Iraq*, No. 3, 1990, p. 20.

[3] *The New York Times*, August 26, 1991, p. 3.

[4] *Wall Street Journal*, August 10, 1990, p. A10.

[5] *MEED*, December 28, 1990, p. 23.

[6] The agricultural trade deficit had reached a peak of $2.4 billion in 1988. U.S. Department of Agriculture—various publications.

[7] *The New York Times*, August 9, 1990, p. D19.

1990, oil prices fell by one-third.[1] Since there were no prospects for any near term significant rise in the volume of exports, this implied a sharp drop in foreign exchange earnings. According to unofficial press reports, in the spring of 1990 Saddam had demanded that oil-rich Arab states provide Iraq with $12 billion to help rebuild its economy and forgive $70 billion in debts.[2] Another press report stated that in July 1990 he told President Mubarak and King Hussein to tell the Gulf states that he needed $30 billion in cash; the "or else" was implied.[3] His public accusations in July, primarily aimed at Kuwait and the UAE, that they were "over-producing" (above the OPEC quotas) and thereby committing "economic aggression" against Iraq, were the precursors of the invasion of Kuwait on August 2.

This is not to suggest that Iraq's economic problems were the sole motivation for its aggression in the summer of 1990—but they were certainly of primary importance. Not long after the invasion, the head of the State Economic Committee told the Iraqi people that with the combined oil exports of Iraq and Kuwait, annual earnings would be $46-60 billion. "I expect that we will be able to repay our debts within two, four or five years at the most. This will be done directly, and without any grace periods or postponements, as we have done in the past. We will place our economy on a sound, healthy basis, and the wheels of development will start moving again."[4] In a televised address to the nation on September 1, the Deputy Prime Minister tried to convince the people that enormous prosperity was in store as a result of the annexation of Kuwait.[5]

---

[1] *EIU: Country Report—Iraq*, No. 3, 1990, p. 15.

[2] *Wall Street Journal*, August 27, 1990, p. A8.

[3] *Wall Street Journal*, August 10, 1990, p. A10.

[4] *MEED*, September 21, 1990, pp. 20-21.

[5] *Business Week*, September 17, 1990, pp. 28-29.

THE PERSIAN GULF WAR AND ITS AFTERMATH

The UN sanctions against trade with Iraq greatly weakened an already weak economy. The air bombardment and the ground war wrought even more serious damage. The U.S.-led coalition ceased hostilities at the end of February 1991, but the embargo on oil shipments was extended indefinitely. Since the Iraqi economy is overwhelmingly dependent on oil revenues, it has continued to retrogress despite the end of the fighting.

In the spring of 1991, Iraqi officials estimated the cost of repairing the physical damage caused by the Gulf War at $150-200 billion.[1] This is probably an exaggeration and may include repairs remaining from the war with Iran. Also, Kuwait has claimed $50-64 billion in reparations in addition to its prewar debt of $14 billion,[2] although it is doubtful that Kuwait can count on collecting very much of that claim. Nonetheless, there is little doubt that the economic burden facing Iraq in this decade is staggering. In addition, economic development has been retarded for a decade, while its population has increased from 13 million in 1980 to 19 million in 1990.[3]

At this writing (spring 1992), UN sanctions continue to effectively embargo Iraqi oil exports. The only small loophole is the shipment of oil to Jordan—about 50 TBD in payment for credits extended by Jordan during the war with Iran. Lacking foreign currency, imports are severely restricted. This greatly hampers industry and agriculture, as well as health and other services. Most of the population is deprived, while a few, including Saddam Hussein and some favored elites, are taking advantage of the runaway inflation and thriving black markets so as to amass huge wealth.[4] In the fall of 1991, the UN agreed to a very partial lifting of sanctions, allowing Iraq to sell oil worth $1.6 billion over the next six months under UN supervision. Of this almost $1 billion would go towards

---

[1] *MidEast Markets*, London, May 27, 1991, p. 3.

[2] *The Middle East*, London, April 1991, p. 40.

[3] IMF, *International Financial Statistics*, various issues.

[4] *Wall Street Journal*, July 15, 1991, p. 1, A8.

financing the import of essential food and medical supplies.[1] So far though, Iraq has refused to accept the UN's terms for this plan.

There is no way of predicting when Iraq will be free to maximize its oil production and exports and to rebuild its shattered economy. One thing is certain: when that occurs, Iraq will extend every effort to exploit its huge oil potential to the maximum. Iraq has ignored OPEC quotas in the past under less pressing circumstances and there can be little doubt that it will do so again.

---

[1] *The Economist,* October 5, 1991, p. 62.

IV IRAN

For Iran, the Kuwait crisis and the severe blows suffered by Iraq were a blessing. Since the mid-1988 cease-fire in its war with Iraq, Iran had restored some of its damaged oil installations. The cessation of exports from Iraq and Kuwait following the invasion in August 1990 opened up new markets for Iranian oil, and at higher prices. Output rose sharply from 2.2 MBD in 1988 to 3.3 MBD in the first half of 1991. Oil export revenues rose rapidly, from $9 billion in 1988 to $14.5 billion in 1991.[1]

Yet, despite the current oil bonanza, Iran's economic situation remains precarious. Iran's gross domestic product (in constant prices) virtually doubled between 1970 and 1977. On a per capita basis the growth was a very respectable 67 percent (7.8 percent per annum). Other sectors (measured by non-oil GDP) expanded even more rapidly, in particular, manufacturing and construction. However, agricultural production advanced more slowly—not much more than the rate of growth of the population—and the agricultural trade deficit widened considerably. On the other hand, private consumption per capita (a measure of living standards) doubled during this period. Moreover, both public and private investment were growing at a high rate. The ratio of gross fixed capital formation to GDP rose from 23 percent in 1970-73 to 31 percent in 1975-78. High levels of investment are usually the harbinger of future economic growth. In short, 1970-77 was a period of high-level prosperity. The engine of growth and

---

[1] *EIU: Country Report—Iran,* No. 2, 1992, p. 6.

prosperity was the oil sector. Oil export revenues in 1977, $23.6 billion, were *ten times those of 1970.* The Shah's government had taken advantage of the 1973-74 oil shock to raise its production from 3.9 MBD in 1970 to 5.7 MBD in 1977, but most of the gain in revenues arose from far higher oil prices.[1]

The Islamic Revolution (1978-79) had, and continues to have, a very disruptive effect on the economy overall. Also, the eight-year war with Iraq (1980-88) dealt severe blows to an already weakened economy. Iran's oil policies in the 1990s will be determined more than in the past by the high priority now given to economic development. These policies will have a strong impact on oil markets during this decade and possibly beyond.

Following Saudi Arabia with its mammoth oil reserves (257 billion barrels), there are four countries with reserves of 90-100 billion barrels each: Iraq, Kuwait, the United Arab Emirates and Iran.[2] While the 3.3 MBD rate of production reached in the first half of 1991 was a post-revolutionary peak, under the Shah output was far higher, ranging between 5.4 and 6.0 MBD in 1973-77. The revolutionary regime had initially adopted a policy of sharply reducing the country's major dependence on oil; Iran's oil production was declining *before* the Iraqi attack in September 1980. However, economic exigencies both during the war and since have forced the government to push for maximum oil production and exports. Recent announcements indicate that Iran plans to increase production capacity to 4 MBD for 1992-1993.[3] The Persian Gulf War has facilitated the realization of this goal. Though Iran's economy is far more diversified than Iraq's, and, *a fortiori,* Saudi Arabia's and the other Gulf states, its dependence on oil exports for foreign exchange earnings is overwhelming. Also financing the importation of machinery and equipment, spare parts and raw materials, is crucial for industry as well as for other sectors. Moreover, Iran has a negative agricultural trade balance. In

---

[1] Unless otherwise stated, the sources for data on Iran's economy are from the IMF, *International Financial Statistics,* and from the annual reports of the Central Bank of Iran.

[2] *BP Statistical Review of World Energy,* June 1991, p. 2.

[3] *Petroleum Intelligence Weekly,* February 24, 1992, p. 4.

other words, it must import food and other essential consumer goods.

IRAN'S ECONOMY—THE REVOLUTION AND THE WAR WITH IRAQ: 1978-88

The economic effects of Iran's revolutionary turmoil were already felt in 1978, before the Shah fled and Khomeini assumed power in February of 1979. In the last months of 1978, strikes and other disruptions reduced oil exports sharply. When exports were resumed in the spring of 1979, they were at a much lower level. The turmoil also affected other sectors. In addition to the many "anti-revolutionaries" killed and imprisoned, there was a mass exodus of managerial classes, professionals, technicians and other skilled people, which greatly weakened the economy. The flight of labor and capital made a bad situation worse, seriously hampering economic development to this day.

The period of revolutionary turmoil between 1978 and 1980 was marked by severe economic retrogression. Oil production declined precipitously from 5.7 MBD in 1977 to 1.5 MBD in 1980. While the escalation in oil prices—triggered by the Iranian revolution—cushioned the decline in revenues, they nonetheless dropped from $23.6 billion in 1977 to $13.3 billion in 1980. Large balance of payments (current account) surpluses were replaced by a large deficit in 1980 ($2.4 billion). In 1980, non-oil GDP was 8 percent lower than in 1977 and investment (gross fixed capital formation) dropped by almost half. Living standards (measured by private consumption per capita) fell by as much as 20 percent during that period, according to official figures.[1]

The economic policies of the revolutionary regime included the expropriation of many larger enterprises. The effects of the exodus of their owners and managers and their replacement by political appointees soon became evident in declining efficiency and deteriorating profitability. What remained of the private sector was subjected to severe restrictions. The revolutionary regime, at least in terms of its

---

[1] This was calculated from the official estimates for private consumption given in the national accounts in current prices, corrected by the official consumer price index and population estimates.

public pronouncements, emphasized self-sufficiency in agriculture and policies to reduce the overwhelming dependence on oil revenues.[1] A wave of nationalizations took place in 1979 involving mainly banks, insurance companies, heavy industries and foreign trade.[2] The attendant economic retrogression demonstrates the disastrous consequences of these policies.

Interestingly enough, following the initial shock of the war with Iraq, the economy showed some signs of improvement. The key again was the oil sector. The volume of oil exports in 1982 and in 1983 was about twice the very low levels of 1980-81 and revenues rose strongly.[3] The authorities permitted a much higher level of (civilian) imports which, in turn, stimulated the economy. Between 1980 and 1985, non-oil GDP rose by 7 percent per annum; while this was half the growth rate of 1969-77 it was nonetheless significant in light of the major diversion of resources to the war effort. The official figures show no significant change in living standards. However, foreign observers believe that the official consumer price index seriously understates the real rate of inflation. *The Financial Times* quoted unofficial estimates of 35 percent inflation in 1984 while the official index showed a rise of only 13 percent.[4] In other words, living standards were continuing to decline even during this period of relative prosperity.

From 1984 on, the Iraqis put a far greater emphasis on economic warfare against Iran, i.e., bombing oil installations, electric power stations and various industrial plants, as well as transportation and communications facilities, and in this they were successful. Despite heroic efforts by the Iranians to restore damaged oil facilities, Iran's oil production was reduced from the relatively high levels of 1982-83. Worse, from Iran's point of view, was the erosion in oil prices. Oil revenues, which had been over $19 billion in 1982 and again in 1983, fell sharply to

---

[1] S. Chubin and C. Tripp, *Iran and Iraq at War* (Boulder: Westview Press, 1988), p. 123.

[2] A. Richards and J. Waterbury, *A Political Economy of the Middle East* (Boulder: Westview Press, 1990), p. 208.

[3] *MEES,* November 19, 1990.

[4] *Financial Times Survey—Iran,* April 1, 1985.

a low of $7.2 billion in 1986. Higher prices raised revenues in the following two years to about $10 billion per annum—about half the level of 1982-83. But these figures underestimate the magnitude of the decline, since Iran was forced to absorb the higher war premiums charged by insurance companies for passage through the Gulf. In other words, net oil revenues suffered an even greater decline.

The authorities in Tehran clamped down strongly on imports, with adverse effects on the economy and on living standards. The official indicators show that for the period 1985-89, non-oil GDP dropped 8 percent, including a 30 percent decline in manufacturing output, a 6 percent contraction in agricultural production, and a similar drop in construction. Investment (gross fixed capital formation) fell by a mammoth 31 percent. These figures bode ill for future economic growth. Living standards suffered another major drop—29 percent, according to official sources, and much more according to unofficial sources.[1] There is little doubt that the rapidly deteriorating economy and rising discontent prompted Khomeini to accept the UN-proposed ceasefire which he had rejected just a few years earlier.

IRAN'S ECONOMY—1990 AND BEYOND

When, following the death of Khomeini, Ali Akbar Hashemi Rafsanjani took over the reins of government in August 1989, the economic picture was grim. The poor performance of agriculture continued in the 1980s despite the priority accorded this sector by the revolutionary ideology. While the revolution had sought to attract millions who had migrated to the cities back to the land, the rural-urban migration increased instead.[2] In the mid-1960s, only 40 percent of the population lived in urban areas; more recently this ratio has risen to about two-thirds. The housing shortage

---

[1] The figures for agriculture are from the U.S. Department of Agriculture, various publications. The other figures are calculated from official Iranian sources.

[2] *Middle East Review*, 1989, p. 72.

became acute, especially in the urban areas.[1] Many of the larger (state-owned) factories were greatly overstaffed and operated at far below capacity. Production was hampered by acute shortages of imported raw materials and spare parts, regular six-hour blackouts in Tehran and in other cities, and shortages of skilled personnel and competent management. The decline in non-oil GDP raised the official unemployment rate (over 25 percent—3.8 million unemployed in 1987)[2] and hidden unemployment even more. An economist at Tehran University estimated that some 3.5 million people were engaged in such dubious occupations as selling government ration coupons and smuggling cigarettes and spare parts, as compared with about one million involved in such activities when the Shah ruled.[3] An unnamed official suggested that the real rate of unemployment, often disguised, was a staggering 43 percent.[4] At the same time there was a serious shortage of skilled technicians and competent managers. In all, the official figures show that living standards in 1989 were 40 percent lower than in 1977. Unofficial estimates of inflation are far higher, indicating a far more severe decline in living standards.

By and large, Rafsanjani has adopted pragmatic policies, more favorable to private enterprise and with fewer governmental controls. However, he faces internal opposition, both from ideological hard-liners as well as from those interest groups who greatly benefit from the corruption and inefficiency which pervade the existing system. The task he faces is formidable—substantially restructuring the economy and achieving sustained high rates of economic growth which would both reduce unemployment from its dangerously high level and improve living standards. With a population of 55 million and growing rapidly, and an economy devastated by revolution and war (as well as some severe earthquakes in recent years) this is no mean task. One observer of Iranian

---

[1] *MEED*, August 9, 1991, pp. 11-12.

[2] *Middle East Review*, 1990, pp. 67-71.

[3] *The Economist*, May 11, 1991, p. 38.

[4] *The Middle East*, April 1991, pp. 34-35.

affairs expressed his belief that "a serious problem will arise if economic growth does not take off in time to prevent popular discontent from spilling over into the streets, which once again would entail a political upheaval, a brain drain, a flight of capital and protracted neglect of industrial sectors."[1] Another report published in the fall of 1991 noted a general feeling of "economic privation and [a] perception that the government is mismanaging the economy and is failing to achieve a fairer distribution of wealth. . . A decline in oil export revenues would slow down economic activity, directly affecting ordinary Iranians. . . [A] series of economic setbacks could lead to social unrest and political upheaval. . . The government is little short of desperate to give the economy a boost as a means of solving its domestic political problems most of which are related to economic difficulties."[2]

In early 1990 the government adopted a five-year plan which would require hard currency expenditures of $112 billion, in addition to much larger local expenditures, emphasizing steel, petrochemicals, as well as an expansion of oil production and refining, electric power and other infrastructural investments. The plan projects that oil export revenues will provide over $80 billion, $10 billion would come from non-oil exports and the balance from foreign loans. The projection that oil revenues would average over $20 billion per annum during the five-year plan was optimistic. The boost of revenues from the Persian Gulf War only pushed oil income to $18.5 billion in 1990 and it then fell to $14.5 billion in 1991.

The increase in oil revenues in 1989, and especially in 1990, permitted the authorities to liberalize import restrictions. As a result, imports rose very sharply from an annual rate of $11 billion in 1986-88 to $17.8 billion in 1990 and a projected $19 billion in 1991.[3] The greater availability of machinery and equipment, spare parts and raw materials, has provided a powerful stimulus to the economy. Estimates for the real growth of the economy are 10 percent in 1990-91 (fiscal year ending March 1991) and 7.5 percent in 1991-92 (fiscal year

---

[1] *EIU: Country Report—Iran*, No. 2, 1990, p. 13.

[2] *EIU: Country Report—Iran*, No. 3, 1991, pp. 4, 18.

[3] *EIU: Country Report—Iran*, No. 3, 1991, pp. 3, 6.

ending March 1992). This compares with the anemic growth of 4 percent in the previous year (barely exceeding the increase in population) and negative growth rates in previous years.

But for Iran to cope with its enormous problems it must have a long period of sustained high rates of economic growth. This will require important changes in economic policies as well as higher oil revenues. It was noted above that the official goal is to raise oil production capacity by about 1.5 MBD to 5.0 MBD by 1993.[1] The strong increase in oil revenues as a consequence of the Persian Gulf War provides Iran with some of the investment capital it needs to expand capacity, and makes it all the more likely that this goal will be achieved. However, Iran's needs are so great that it already seeking to expand oil exports even more in the next few years. Iran is not likely to pay much attention to OPEC quotas once it achieves the capacity to exceed them. Tehran's desperate need for oil revenues has important implications for future oil markets, as well as for economic developments in the region.

---

[1] *Petroleum Intelligence Weekly*, April 8, 1991, p. 10.

V OTHER OPEC STATES

This study has thus far focused on four major Middle East oil exporters, Saudi Arabia, Kuwait, Iraq and Iran, analyzing the changes in their economies and finances, and their drive to increase the volume of oil exports in order to earn more revenues. For the first three, the Persian Gulf War raised future financial needs to far higher dimensions. In the case of Iran, with its much larger and rapidly growing population, the dismal state of its economy in the aftermath of the 1979 revolution and the 1980-88 war with Iraq compel the authorities to maximize oil production as rapidly as possible. Huge oil reserves in all four countries will permit much higher levels of production. While, since the mid-1980s, all have, at one time or another, "violated" OPEC quotas, in recent years other OPEC states have also been rapidly expanding their productive capacity with the United Arab Emirates (UAE) being the most extreme offender.

THE UNITED ARAB EMIRATES (UAE)

The United Arab Emirates' oil reserves, estimated at 98 billion barrels, are of the same order of magnitude as those of Iraq, Iran and Kuwait. With a population of less than two million, of whom three-fourths are foreigners, why the avid desire for more oil revenues? The answer lies mainly in the UAE's unique political structure. It is a loose federation of seven quasi-independent Emirates, with a federal government dependent on the subventions of Abu Dhabi, by far the richest member, and, to a much lesser extent, on Dubai. The other five members have little or no oil, and oil revenues accrue to the individual Emirates, not the federal government, which is the chief conduit of aid to the five poor members of the federation. The poorer Emirates have been increasingly exerting pressure on Abu Dhabi to augment its contributions to the national treasury. Moreover, in recent years the UAE allocated as much as 40 percent of its oil revenues to finance higher expenditures on the military and on internal security.[1] In view of its small population it may come as a surprise that in every year between 1984 and 1988 the consolidated budget of the UAE (the federal budget plus Abu Dhabi's and Dubai's) was in deficit.[2]

Since the mid-1980s there has been a strong and successful drive to raise production. Between 1984 and the first half of 1990, production almost doubled, rising from 1.1 to 2.1 MBD. The shutdown of Iraqi and Kuwaiti exports during the Gulf crisis permitted the UAE to raise production further, reaching a capacity in 1991 of 2.36 MBD. But while the crisis enabled the UAE to expand its revenues, it also made additional demands on its treasury to help finance the war and to compensate those countries participating in the anti-Iraq coalition.[3] Given its huge oil reserves, there is no doubt that these expansion plans are feasible, and that the UAE authorities will extend every effort to implement them.

LIBYA

Between 1981 and 1989 Libyan output was an almost static 1-1.1 MBD. At the same time, however, declining prices reduced its revenues very sharply, from a peak of $22 billion in 1980 to less than $6 billion per annum in 1986-88. Despite stringent import restrictions (which adversely affected its economy) there were sizeable balance of payments (current account) deficits between 1981 and 1988, other than in 1985. The **cumulative** deficits between 1981 and 1988 were almost $10 billion dollars.[4] U.S. sanctions barring American companies

---

[1] *Financial Times Survey—United Arab Emirates*, March 24, 1988, p. 1.

[2] *IMF Survey*, August 7, 1989, p. 242.

[3] *MEED*, April 19, 1991, p. iii.

[4] *International Financial Statistics,* various issues.

from operating in Libya and proscribing oil imports from that country were important factors in restraining Libyan production.

Libya also took advantage of the Kuwait crisis to increase its output from 1.1 MBD in 1989 to 1.5 MBD in the first half of 1991—thus reaching the limit of its capacity. A foreign oil man working in Libya reported that in the spring of 1991 "the Libyans begged and begged us to produce more oil, but there just wasn't the capacity any more."[1] Since 1988 Libya has offered more favorable terms to oil companies, and eight have signed agreements for exploration and development. It is projected that by the mid-1990s, 550 TBD will be added to capacity.[2] And there is no sign yet that, in its effort to punish Libya's support for terrorism, the international community would be willing to target Libya's oil industry.

VENEZUELA

Venezuela is the foremost OPEC producer outside the Middle East. While during the 1970s and until the mid-1980s, production was in a downtrend, recent years have seen a reversal, with output rising from 1.7 MBD in 1985-87 to over 2.0 MBD in the first half of 1990. Like all others with spare capacity, Venezuela also took advantage of the Kuwait crisis to raise output to 2.4 MBD in the first half of 1991, which was close to capacity. Moreover, Venezuela has ambitious plans to expand capacity to 3.5 MBD by 1995 and to add another million barrels per day by the following year.[3]

Despite its far more diversified economy (as compared with the Arab Gulf states) Venezuela depends on oil for some 90 percent of its export revenues. The decline in oil revenues during the 1980s had a strong recessionary impact on its economy. Austerity measures led to serious riots in February

---

[1] *The Economist,* March 23, 1991, p. 45.

[2] *Middle East Economic Survey,* March 5, 1990 pp. A1, A4; *Petroleum Economist,* April 1991, pp. 6-7.

[3] *Wall Street Journal,* May 6, 1991, p. A9; *Petroleum Intelligence Weekly,* June 24, 1991, p.1.

1989 in which roughly 300 people were killed.[1] The reversal in its oil policy since the later 1980s, favoring a more rapid development of its resources, is a consequence of this economic distress.

The head of the Venezuelan oil company stated in October 1990 that his country's expansion plans were based on its very large reserves of hydrocarbons, including 59 billion barrels of conventional oil reserves, 270 billion barrels of bitumens (sometimes called superheavy crude), and large reserves of natural gas. He said that new techniques were being developed to convert bitumens into petroleum products and thus transform Venezuela "into the first oil power in the world." His agenda was to persuade his government that its OPEC quota "was not working for the interests of Venezuela."[2] Venezuela has, in fact, exceeded its quota in recent years (though not nearly as flagrantly as the UAE and Kuwait) since abiding by OPEC restrictions would seriously impair the realizations of its ambitious goals. Shortly after the invasion of Kuwait, the manager of the Venezuelan state oil company asserted: "When you are buying the cheap oil of the Middle East, you are not calculating the cost of defending the Middle East [oil supplies]."[3] The intended audience for this pronouncement was the U.S. political leadership, who he had hoped would favor Venezuelan oil over Middle Eastern oil.

Another report from Venezuela spoke of a new technique, namely, a mixture of bitumen and water emulsion that is liquid and easy to handle like oil but priced like coal. This mixture had been tested for two years in power plants in Canada, the UK and Japan. A study by the *Financial Times Management Report* concluded that its potential in the energy market is "awesome."[4] There may be a measure of hyperbole here, but clearly Venezuela has the resource base for a more rapid development of its oil resources and the determination to exploit them more fully. Recent reports indicate that the

---

[1] *The New York Times*, August 24, 1990, p. D4.

[2] *MEES*, October 29, 1990, pp. A2, A3.

[3] *The New York Times*, August 30, 1990, pp. D1, D7.

[4] *The New York Times*, October 15, 1990, p. D1.

commercial extraction of bitumens has been initiated, and a number of major Western companies have signed up to examine the feasibility of converting bitumens into gasoline.[1] There is good reason to believe that during the course of this decade Venezuela's ambitious expansion plans will have a strong and growing impact on world oil markets.

In the 1970s, Venezuela, like Libya and many other Third World oil producers, espoused the nationalization of oil resources and viewed Western oil companies as the front-line troops of Western imperialism. Now, however, Venezuela and its fellow oil producers favor cooperation with foreign firms and offer them attractive terms to induce them to participate in the exploitation of their oil resources. The economic hardships which these countries have endured, especially since the mid-1980s (when oil prices fell sharply), have persuaded them to become more realistic. These countries have neither adequate investment capital nor the up-to-date technology which the Western firms can offer. **The bankruptcy of socialism has made it easier for the leaders of these countries to reverse course and to invite the participation of foreign firms in the exploration and development of their oil resources. This is occurring not only in Venezuela but worldwide.** And, this change has very important ramifications for world oil markets.

NIGERIA AND INDONESIA

Nigeria's economy is weighed down by a large external debt and it, too, has raised oil production since the mid-1980s, from 1.2 MBD in 1983 to 1.7 MBD in 1989. It also took advantage of the Kuwait crisis to raise production by another 200 TBD. Moreover, it plans to raise capacity to 2.5 MBD by 1995.[2] Indonesia also raised its output by 240 TBD (first half of 1991 compared with the same period in 1990). Texaco and Chevron are spending $2 billion to build the world's largest steam recovery operation at the Duri oil field in Indonesia,

---

[1] *Newsweek,* October 21, 1991, p. 62.

[2] *Financial Times,* February 19, 1991, p. 2.

which should boost production by over 250 TBD by 1995.[1] Both Nigeria and Indonesia have had to "reschedule" foreign debts in recent years and their drive to increase oil exports stems from their financial problems.[2] Mass rioting in Nigeria underscores the acuteness of this country's economic situation.

---

[1] *Fortune*, April 22, 1991, p. 144.

[2] *Euromoney—Petroleum Economist*, Special Supplement, June-July 1990, p. 81.

VI THE WAR'S EFFECT ON EGYPT, SYRIA AND JORDAN

Though they are not major oil producers, the economic fortunes of Syria and Egypt are tied to OPEC, and Jordan, which has no oil to speak of, also benefitted greatly from the oil-boom in the Gulf states.

In retribution for Egyptian President Hosni Mubarak's support of the U.S.-led coalition, Saddam Hussein ordered the expulsion of hundreds of thousands of Egyptians who had been working in Iraq and in Kuwait. The consequence was the loss of hundreds of millions of dollars in remittances which the workers had been sending home, aggravating the already serious problem of unemployment. Although Egypt was very far from the war zone, tourism declined drastically, and there was also a drop in Suez Canal revenues, another important source of foreign exchange earnings. On the other hand, Egypt gained from the higher oil prices triggered by the war. Oil export revenues in 1990-91 were $850 million higher than in the prior year, though the volume of exports was substantially unchanged.[1] Overall the impact of the war on Egypt's economy was a net loss of about $2.5 billion.[2]

The compensation Egypt received from the U.S. and its allies was many multiples of its losses. Egypt's foreign debt had grown by leaps and bounds, from $4.4 billion in 1974 to $21.5

---

[1] See Appendices—Table 5.

[2] *The Middle East*, June 1991, p. 3; *EIU: Country Report—Egypt*, No. 4, 1990, p. 11.

billion in 1980 and $46.1 billion in 1990.[1] Other estimates were higher—$52 billion in 1990.[2] Before the war arrears on debt payments had reached an estimated $18 billion, including payments due on the military debt owed to the U.S.[3] Following the invasion of Kuwait and Egypt's participation in the anti-Iraq coalition, the U.S. forgave about $7 billion in military debts, and Saudi Arabia and the other Gulf states forgave a similar amount. The so-called Paris Club of creditors, including the U.S. and Gulf states, agreed to forgive debts totaling $25 billion, and others were rescheduled. The consequence: debt service (annual payments on account of principal and interest) was reduced sharply from about $5.5 to 1.5 billion.[4] In addition, Egypt was the beneficiary of generous grants and soft loans from the Gulf states and Europe. Grants received in fiscal year 1990-91 (beginning July 1, 1990) were $4.7 billion, as compared with $1.1 billion in the prior year. For the first time in over two decades the balance of payments (the current account) ended up on the plus side.[5] In addition, with the prodding of the U.S. government, the International Monetary Fund, after years of negotiations, finally came to an agreement with Egypt calling for economic reforms in return for IMF and World Bank loans.

Before the war, Egypt's economy had been going from bad to worse. *The Financial Times* had given the following description:

"An unmanageable foreign debt of $50 billion, overdependence on foreign aid, limited employment opportunities, an unwieldy (massive) bureaucracy, a chronically inefficient state sector, and perhaps, most critically, a despondency among the young about

---

[1] See Appendices—Table 5.

[2] *Middle East Monitor,* February 1991, p. 22.

[3] *The Middle East,* January 1991, p. 30.

[4] *MEED,* June 7, 1991, p. 24.

[5] See Appendices—Table 5.

an uncertain future . . . The country is sliding deeper into recession."[1]

Another analyst concluded:

"The economy is Egypt's critical battleground . . . [T]he portents are ominous . . . [T]he unemployment rate is over 20 percent . . . this is a potentially explosive situation . . . [There is] a continuing deterioration of the economy . . . [U]nemployment and inflation have reached levels that should be warning signals . . . Egypt's stagflationary problems require a bold new approach . . . The question is whether the leadership has the will or the imagination."[2]

The massive debt forgiveness and foreign aid which Egypt received as a reward for its support of the anti-Iraq coalition was fortuitous. As one Western economist suggested, only half in jest, "the Egyptians should erect a statue to Saddam Hussein in [Cairo's central] Tahrir Square."[3] Egypt's economy and its leadership have been granted a reprieve. The question is: what are the longer term prospects? Concretely, will sustained economic growth replace stagnation, provide productive jobs for the unemployed and underemployed, and improve living standards for the tens of millions living below the poverty line?

EGYPT'S ECONOMIC STRUCTURE

The American embassy in Cairo noted in its 1988 report that the Egyptian economy had been stagnant since 1985 and concluded that: "The preeminent economic challenge confronting Egypt remains the need to stimulate growth and productivity. Egypt has vast resources—fifty million people, fertile land and excellent climate, generous endowments of hydrocarbons (oil and gas) and minerals—but the efficiency of their utilization is low. Egypt's tradition of centralized planning, reliance on the public sector, and government

---

[1] *Financial Times Survey—Egypt,* April 4, 1990, p. 31.

[2] *Middle East Review,* 1989, pp. 59-63.

[3] *Financial Times Survey—Egypt,* June 24, 1991, p. ii.

controls of economic activity dates from the 1950s."[1] The latter reference is to the economic system called "Arab Socialism," which Gamal Abdul Nasser adopted in the later 1950s and which has been modified only marginally by his successors, Anwar Sadat (1970-1981) and Hosni Mubarak.

Under Nasser, there was large-scale nationalization of all large private enterprises. At the same time the people were promised cheap food and other essentials, as well as free education and health care. The government dealt with the problem of unemployment by ordering public sector enterprises to hire large numbers of unneeded workers, and the managers of these enterprises had no power to dismiss unproductive workers or to set wage levels. University graduates, in particular, were promised positions in the bureaucracy, which naturally enough, mushroomed. Tens of thousands flocked to the universities, which were tuition-free, and which promised secure lifetime jobs to the graduates. More corruption and inefficiency were the almost inevitable results. Concomitantly, state enterprises required large direct or, more often, hidden subsidies, and cash transfusions from the treasury to balance the books and maintain operations. In order to keep prices of food and other essentials from rising, subsidies on those items were regularly increased. Budgetary deficits rose sharply, adding to inflationary pressures and/or balance of payments deficits. Agriculture remained private but was tightly controlled—with adverse results. Egypt had its first agricultural trade deficit (farm exports minus farm imports) in 1974, at $224 million. By 1988, the deficit had reached $4.4 billion.[2]

Under Sadat there were few changes until after the 1973 Yom Kippur War and the resulting oil shock. Sadat's "Open Door" policy aimed at some liberalization of the economy and invited private enterprise, both foreign and domestic. In reality, to the extent that private enterprise invested, it was largely in trade, finance and tourism. There was little private investment in industry. Powerful interest groups resisted investment in private industry in those areas which might compete with and

---

[1] U.S. Department of Commerce, *Foreign Economic Trends—Egypt,* May 1988, pp. 5-8.

[2] See Appendices—Table 7.

undermine state enterprises. Under Sadat consumer subsidies rose to far higher levels, along with transfers to the inefficient public sector, and the bureaucracy grew to even more massive dimensions.

During the latter half of the 1970s, the economy did well and living standards rose, but for the most part this was due to external factors, mainly oil. In the mid-1970s Egypt became a net oil exporter. It is noteworthy that even under Nasser, who espoused a nationalist and socialist philosophy, the oil sector was an exception. Western oil companies entered into agreements with Egypt, and oil production rose rapidly from 11.7 million tons (235 TBD) in 1975 to 31 million tons (620 TBD) in 1980-81. Since this was a period of rapidly rising prices, oil export revenues rose sharply from a mere $315 million in 1975 to $2.9 billion in 1980-81. To put this figure into perspective, it might be noted that all other commodity exports, including cotton, were only $1.1 billion in the latter year. The Suez Canal was reopened in 1975, and toll fees reached $780 million in 1980-81. This was due, in part, to oil tankers transiting the canal to Europe and America, and the oil boom in the Gulf countries which stimulated growing imports from the West, also through the canal.[1]

But the single most important change was the migration of millions of Egyptians to work in the Gulf states and the remittances they sent home to their families. Official estimates show a precipitous rise from a mere $188 million in 1974 to $2.9 billion in 1980-81—equal to oil export revenues in the latter year.[2] However, the Egyptians abroad sent many more billions of dollars through unofficial channels, unrecorded in the official estimates of the balance of payments. The exodus of millions of workers also eased the problem of unemployment. Tourism, much of which was from the rich Arab Gulf states, picked up rapidly after 1973. Following the conclusion of the Camp David agreements in 1979, U.S. aid was substantially increased. The overall prosperity is evident from the fact that

---

[1] See Appendices—Tables 5 and 7.

[2] See Appendices—Table 5.

living standards (measured by real private consumption per capita) rose by over 50 percent between 1974 and 1980-81.[1]

What is clear is that the prosperity Egypt enjoyed in the latter half of the 1970s and early 1980s was, for the most part, oil-related. The timing of the assassination of Sadat was unfortunate. Oil prices peaked in 1981 and then dropped sharply. During the first half of the 1980s Egypt's oil production did rise, but far more slowly, and between 1985 and 1990 it was stagnant. At the same time, domestic oil consumption continued to rise rapidly, leaving a smaller export surplus, while world oil prices were dropping. The very low domestic prices for oil products—one-fourth of comparable international prices—stimulated the rapid growth in consumption. Oil export revenues fell from a peak of over $3 billion in 1981-82 to $1.3 billion in 1989-90.

Suez Canal revenues continued to expand during that period, but far more slowly, as was the case with tourism. According to official records, workers' remittances reached a peak of $3.9 billion in 1984-85 and then declined in the following years.[2] However, it is possible that more remittances were transferred through unofficial channels as the gap between the legal exchange rate and the black (free) market rate widened. In any case it is clear that, on the whole, the main sources of Egyptian prosperity in the latter half of the 1970s and early 1980s had weakened since the mid-1980s. Thus, the economy was mainly dependent for growth and prosperity on its traditional sectors—agriculture and manufacturing.

Estimates by the U.S. Department of Agriculture show that Egypt's per capita farm production fell or was stagnant during the latter half of the 1970s and in the 1980s.[3] As noted earlier, the agriculture trade deficit rose precipitously. Egypt now imports some 60 percent of its food requirements.[4] The

---

[1] See Appendices—Table 7.

[2] See Appendices—Table 5.

[3] See Appendices—Table 7.

[4] U.S. Embassy in Cairo, *Report of the Agricultural Counselor*, February 1990, p. 4.

problems in Egypt's agriculture sector stem from adverse policies. For many years the government had set the procurement price of cotton and some other farm products far below international levels.[1] Instead of providing incentives to produce more, the government effectively instituted disincentives.

The outlook for the industrial sector, dominated by the state enterprises, is even less hopeful. The Egyptian economy has been described as "the sick man" of the Middle East and its industrial sector as "the sick man of the Egyptian economy."[2] The root of the problem is public sector manufacturing enterprises, riddled with inefficiency, corruption, overstaffing, and large losses, which are directly or indirectly covered by the treasury. Industrial exports, measured in constant dollars, have been stagnant for many years.

In order to minimize overt unemployment, the government has added more and more people to the bureaucracy. The civil service numbered about 3.5 million people in 1990 (about one-fourth of the labor force), more than double its 1974 figure. These figures do not include the public sector enterprises, which also suffer from extreme overstaffing, nor do they include the military services.[3] Subsidies, direct and indirect, have added to the drain on the treasury. The budgetary deficit as a ratio of gross domestic product averaged 20 percent between 1974 and 1980-81, and about the same throughout the 1980s.[4] The gap was partly covered by foreign loans and the balance by internal borrowing. By way of comparison, in LDCs as a whole, deficits averaged 5-6 percent in the 1980s.[5] The huge deficits persisted in the 1980s, despite the fact that military expenditures (as a ratio of GDP) had been

---

[1] D.J. Sullivan, "The Political Economy of Reform in Egypt," *International Journal for Middle East Studies*, August 1990, p. 324.

[2] *The Financial Times Survey—Egypt*, July 20, 1980, p. iv; June 17, 1991, p. 13.

[3] *MEED*, June 8, 1990, p. 20.

[4] See Appendices—Table 6.

[5] IMF, *International Financial Statistics Yearbook*, 1990, pp. 156-157.

substantially reduced.[1] Despite substantial grants from the U.S. and others, the deficits in the balance on current account (of the balance of payments) rose in the 1980s. The result was an escalating foreign debt.[2]

EGYPT'S ECONOMIC OUTLOOK

The key question for Egypt is whether its leadership will take advantage of the recent large-scale debt reductions and the bonanza in foreign aid to bring about a radical restructuring of its economy, which over time could stimulate economic growth, jobs and incomes, while reducing inflation and other economic ills. The record does not leave much room for optimism.

In the latter half of the 1970s and early 1980s, Egypt benefitted from a plethora of foreign exchange earnings, plus foreign aid, but did little to alter the basic economic structure and policies which inhibited economic growth and stimulated consumption. Once these exogenous stimuli were attenuated, the economy was again in deep trouble. Moreover, the oil boom in the Gulf states provided jobs, as well as much higher incomes, to millions of Egyptians. There are varying estimates as to the number of Egyptians working abroad. One estimate is that at the peak in 1985 they totaled 2.8 million, of which one million were in Iraq, about 140,000 in Jordan, and the others in Saudi Arabia, the other Gulf states, and Libya. The daunting task facing Egypt is to provide **productive jobs** for the hundreds of thousands entering the labor force each year, for the millions unemployed (estimated at some 20 percent of the labor force before the Persian Gulf War) plus those millions of who are ostensibly employed in the civil service and the public sector enterprises, as well as for the returnees from Iraq and Kuwait.

The IMF agreement finally concluded in the spring of 1991 called for some important reforms, including sharp reductions in budgetary deficits; much lower food subsidies; a more realistic pricing system to include raising energy prices to

---

[1]According to estimates of the U.S. Arms Control and Disarmament Agency. See Appendices—Table 6.

[2] See Appendices—Table 2.

international levels; the removal of price controls; the abolition of compulsory government procurement of various farm products at low prices; a uniform foreign exchange rate; and higher interest rates. It was also expected that privatization of the public sector enterprises would proceed. All of these reforms are essential. But the question remains: are they sufficient, and, more important, will they be implemented?

Powerful interest groups will continue to resist radical changes, especially where their jobs, powers or privileges are at stake. The government bureaucracy, which is charged with implementing reforms, strongly resists and sabotages change. In a moment of frustration with the bureaucracy the president lamented that it "seeks to make the easy difficult and the possible impossible."[1] Indeed, by all accounts, Mubarak has made little headway in lessening the stultifying effects of the bureaucracy.[2]

In July 1989 Mubarak, for the first time, publicly endorsed the principle of privatization. But then, a month later, under fire from those with a vested interest in the public sector—government officials, managers, and workers in the state enterprises—he backed off, stating that profitable businesses should be kept, loss-making ones would, in any case, be hard to sell, while "strategic" industries must be kept in the public sector.[3] That does not leave much room for privatization. Those private industries that have been established are often frustrated by the maze of regulations. For instance, General Motors, which produces trucks and buses in Egypt, is not allowed to change product mix without permission, nor is it allowed to produce more than 18,200 vehicles a year. These regulations are designed to protect state-owned plants from competition.[4] An American economist calls Egypt's regulation of private enterprise a "nightmare."[5]

---

[1] *The New York Times*, November 12, 1989, p. 16.

[2] *The New York Times*, November 11, 1990, p. 14.

[3] *MidEast Markets*, November 27, 1989, p. 12.

[4] *Financial Times Survey—Egypt*, April 4, 1990, p. 32.

[5] *The Middle East*, June 1991, p. 38.

Implementing the reform program will be a herculean task. It means—at least for a number of years—still higher rates of inflation (as subsidies are reduced), even more massive unemployment (as unneeded or unproductive workers are dismissed by the public sector enterprises and the civil service), and falling living standards. The IMF official who signed the agreement with Egypt expressed his belief that, assuming the reforms are implemented, it will take three or four years before an economic upturn takes place.[1] But can the leadership cope with the discontent, if not worse, which these reforms will surely generate at least in the short run? The example of history is not encouraging.

In 1977, under prodding from the IMF, Sadat announced a sharp reduction in food subsidies, which meant much higher prices for bread and other food products. This provoked mass rioting and many were killed; the following day most of the price increases were rescinded. This event, which has never been forgotten by Egypt's leaders, makes them recoil from taking drastic measures. Analysts in Egypt fear that Mubarak may use relief from the heavy debt burden and the inflow of large-scale foreign aid to avoid unpopular measures, rather than implement them.[2]

The Persian Gulf War gave Egypt's economy a shot in the arm, but the longer term outlook does not look favorable. In the 1970s and early 1980s, oil came to the rescue, yet barring major new oil finds, the outlook is for declining Egyptian output. Indeed, one international oil executive predicts that in fifteen years Egypt will become a net oil importer.[3] The prospects of another oil boom coming to the rescue are dim. As one analyst concluded, "Egypt can be a dangerous place for . . . optimists with short memories."[4]

---

[1] *EIU: Country Report—Egypt*, No. 2, 1991, p. 10.

[2] *The New York Times*, November 11, 1990, p. 14.

[3] *Petroleum Intelligence Weekly*, May 27, 1991, pp. 4-5.

[4] *Financial Times Survey—Egypt*, June 24, 1991, p. i.

THE PERSIAN GULF WAR AND SYRIA'S ECONOMY

In many respects Syria's economic policies and problems are similar to those of Egypt, but there are important differences. Syria, too, adopted "Arab socialism" in the later 1950s and 1960s, and, in fact, these policies were initiated during the period of union with Egypt—the United Arab Republic (1958-61). The drive to nationalize industrial and other enterprises was intensified following the breakup of the union in 1961. Inevitably, economic growth lagged in the 1960s and problems intensified. Hafez Assad, who assumed the presidency in 1970, made some modifications, (the so-called "corrective revolution"), but the basic structure and policies favoring the public sector and centralized controls remained in place.

There was some improvement when oil began to flow in Syria—albeit on a small scale—in 1968. Then, following the first oil shock in 1973-74, there was a period of rapid economic growth fueled by much more generous aid from the rich Arab countries; growing remittances from Syrians working in these countries; and much higher dues from the pipelines from Iraq and Saudi Arabia transiting Syria, as well as Syria's own rising oil production and exports. The large inflow of foreign exchange permitted the authorities to liberalize imports of capital as well as consumer goods. Investment rose very strongly in industry, housing, transport and communications.

Following the boom there was a period of economic stagnation in 1976-78 mainly because the Iraqis closed the pipeline (they had built alternative routes through Turkey and the Gulf); Syrian oil production began to decline; and military outlays rose rapidly when it sent troops into Lebanon in 1976 not long after the civil war in that country had erupted. But the second oil shock, 1979-80, soon came to the rescue—for a while. While Syria's oil production continued to drop, far higher international prices raised annual oil export revenues from about $650 million in 1975-78 to $1.6 billion in 1980-82.[1]

---

[1] See Syria—Tables 10 and 11. For details and sources see Eliyahu Kanovsky, "What's Behind Syria's Current Economic Problems?" in H. Shaked and D. Dishon eds., *Middle East Contemporary Survey*, Vol. VIII, (Boulder: Westview Press, 1986). Table 11 shows a small oil trade balance, but from 1982 to 1988 Syria was receiving oil shipments from Iran, partly on a grant basis, and partly as a long-term, no-interest loan.

Grants from the Arab oil states rose sharply to an annual average of $1.7 billion in 1979-81, more than double grants received in 1976-78, and Syria was also the recipient of soft loans (long-term low-interest loans). The oil boom in the Gulf states attracted many more Syrian workers, and remittances rose accordingly.[1] Between 1979 and 1983 real gross domestic product (GDP) rose by an average annual rate of 5.6 percent per annum, or 2.2 percent per capita. Growth was far less than in 1974-76, but was, nonetheless, positive.

1983 marked the beginning of a longer and deeper recession. Official data, which tend to underestimate inflation, exaggerate real growth and understate declines, show an absolute drop in GDP until 1987. On a per capita basis, 1987's GDP was 16 percent lower than in 1983—a severe decline. According to official estimates, living standards (measured by real private consumption per capita) had plunged precipitously—by over half—between 1981 and 1987.[2] Inflation was 36 percent in 1986 and 60 percent in 1987—according to official estimates. Unofficial estimates were far higher, from 50-100 percent.[3] Foreign aid from rich Arab states was diminishing and the external debt was growing, reaching almost $5 billion in 1988, **not** including a $15 billion military debt owed to the Soviet Union. In 1986 the World Bank suspended its aid because of arrears in payments on earlier loans.[4] Arms imports had risen strongly and military budgets were the equivalent of about 20 percent of GDP in 1983-86, (not including arms imports). Agricultural production shows wide annual fluctuations, depending on weather conditions, but the overall performance was poor and output lagged behind

---

Syria was exporting its own oil and used the Iranian oil for refining for domestic consumption.

[1] Estimates of remittances are notoriously unreliable because most are transferred through unofficial channels. There is a strong presumption that transfers through the black or free market rose strongly in the 1980s, since the gap between the official and black market rates was widening.

[2] See Appendices—Table 10.

[3] See Appendices—Table 10; *EIU: Country Report—Syria,* No. 1, 1987, p. 14.

[4] *Mideast Markets,* May 30, 1988, p. 4.

population growth. Production in the manufacturing sector declined in 1985-88, partly a consequence of the overall inefficiency of the public sector enterprises and partly because of import restrictions imposed by the authorities to conserve foreign exchange. Severe shortages of imported raw materials and spare parts hampered production in industry as well as in other sectors.[1]

An economist visiting Syria in 1986 said that basic necessities like coffee, sugar, and flour were in short supply, electric power was cut off for six hours each day, and water was shut off at night. Summing up the situation, he said: "It's a zany picture of East European socialism and Levantine capitalism . . . You have the inefficiency and low-level corruption of socialism plus the rake-offs and high-level corruption of the Levant . . . If things continue to decline as sharply, perhaps in ten years they might approach . . . present-day Egypt."[2] Another report published in 1988 noted: "The majority of the population [is] faced with drastically reduced standards of living which are now beginning to affect even the middle class . . . [A] minority with the right political, social and bureaucratic connections . . . increases its wealth prodigiously . . . [and] unabashedly flaunts [its] wealth, and, for the first time, the poor are to be found rummaging in rubbish . . . looking for food."[3]

The American Embassy in Damascus estimated in 1986 that unemployment had reached 20 percent, not including much hidden unemployment, especially in the public sector, and that inflation rates had risen to 100 percent. Smuggling, largely from Lebanon "with the complicity of Syrian military and civil authorities," had reached enormous dimensions estimated at $1 billion per annum. This compares with $2 billion in officially recorded imports of commodities, excluding oil, in 1986. The American Embassy's evaluation: "The problem is not that the Syrian economy is poor or backward; [but that] it is performing far below potential . . . [W]ere the government to embark on reform, the resulting

---

[1] See Appendices—Tables 10 and 11.

[2] *The New York Times*, December 3, 1986, p. A4.

[3] *The Middle East*, November 1988, p. 11.

dislocations would be extremely wrenching" and strongly opposed by powerful interest groups.[1] Very large military expenditures made a bad situation worse. The Soviet Defense Minister, visiting Syria in March 1989, observed that "Syria's military capabilities are much bigger than [its] economic and demographic weight . . . can handle."[2]

Large-scale smuggling from Lebanon, in which the armed forces are heavily involved, makes up for some of the shortages in Syria—for those who can afford the price. Much of the financing comes from the drug traffic and the Bekaa Valley, which is under Syrian control, is the source of hashish and heroin. In 1989, the U.S. Drug Enforcement Administration estimated Syrian profits from drug trafficking at $1 billion a year. According to a DEA report: "Almost the entire Syrian government is involved in the drug business . . . Syrian army trucks, helicopters and vessels are used routinely to transport drugs to Damascus International Airport, to exit points along the Turkish border, and to Syrian ports."[3] Another report in a Middle Eastern journal noted that "Syrian army officers [are] engaged in trading narcotics for consumer goods . . . [E]ver since the Syrians moved into the Bekaa Valley in 1976, drug traffic has prospered under the sponsorship of high-ranking Syrian officers . . . One banking source estimates the value of the [narcotics] business at $5 billion a year . . . The military has grown fat on the proceeds."[4] It is not hard to understand why Syrian army officers are eager to be stationed in Lebanon.[5]

In the later 1980s there was, again, an improvement in the Syrian economy mainly for one reason—oil. A major new

---

[1] U.S. Department of State, *Report from U.S. Embassy in Damascus*, 1986.

[2] *The Middle East*, July 1989, pp. 34-35. On the effect of Syria's military expansion in its economy, see Patrick Clawson, *Unaffordable Ambitions: Syria's Military Build-Up and Economic Crisis*, Policy Paper No. 17, (Washington D.C.: The Washington Institute for Near East Policy, 1989).

[3] *The New York Times*, October 28, 1990, P. E19.

[4] *The Middle East*, March 1990, p. 46.

[5] *The Middle East*, September 1991, p. 21.

field was discovered in the northeast by a consortium of Western companies, yielding oil of superior quality.[1] Production rose rapidly from 160-180 TBD in 1977-85 to 400 TBD in 1990. Net oil export revenues (exports minus imports of crude oil and products) rose sharply, reaching $1.1 billion in 1989 and almost $1.5 dollars in 1990.[2] Part of the increase in revenues in 1990 was due to the higher prices prevailing following the invasion of Kuwait. The uptrend was continuing in 1991 when production was approaching 500 TBD.[3]

The resulting availability of foreign exchange permitted the authorities to increase imports of machinery and equipment, raw materials and spare parts. Many enterprises which had been operating far below capacity were now able to raise production, and the government also embarked on some major investment projects including communications, iron and steel, textiles and fertilizers. However, there is no indication of moves to bring about basic structural reforms. In fact, the relative abundance of foreign exchange eases the pressure on the leadership to implement far-reaching changes in economic policies.[4] A high government official said pointedly, in 1991, that economic liberalization will not include privatization and as of the summer of 1992 this seems to still be the case.[5]

SYRIA'S ECONOMY AND THE GULF WAR

The Gulf War was a net plus for Syria's economy. Over 100,000 Syrians who had been in Kuwait were expelled by Saddam Hussein, with a resulting loss of some $200 million in remittances.[6] On the other hand, Syria gained considerably

---

[1] *MEED*, October 12, 1984, p. 50.

[2] See Appendices—Tables 10 and 11; *EIU: Country Report—Syria*, No. 3, 1991, pp. 3-4.

[3] *Petroleum Economist*, September 1991, p. 7.

[4] *MEED*, September 27, 1991, pp. 4-5.

[5] *EIU: Country Report—Syria*, No. 3, 1991, p. 4.

[6] *The Economist*, October 13, 1990, p. 43.

from the higher oil prices prevailing since the invasion of Kuwait. Furthermore, aid from the rich Arab states, which had been dwindling before the war, rose strongly since Syria announced its participation in the anti-Iraq coalition. Japan and a number of European countries joined Saudi Arabia and Kuwait in offering Syria substantial financial aid.[1] According to *The Economist,* Syria received $2 billion from the Gulf states, "money it promptly spent on weapons."[2]

Syria's Oil Minister stated in 1991 that he expects increased exploration will triple production "within the next few years" from its current level of close to one half MBD.[3] His expectations may well be overly optimistic (the projected amount of oil to be produced in 1992 is only a little more than one half MBD), but the uptrend is unmistakable.[4] However, if oil prices, as may be anticipated, decline, this will offset, at least in part, the growth in the volume of exports. But the failure to implement far-reaching economic reforms implies that, following the current oil boom, the economy will again stagnate—as was the case following the oil shocks of the 1970s and early 1980s. The above-mentioned increase in Syrian military spending may possibly be affordable today, but in the longer run can only make a bad situation worse.

THE KUWAIT CRISIS AND JORDAN'S ECONOMY

Though Jordan's oil production is minuscule, its economy was massively affected by the oil boom and subsequent crash in the neighboring countries. Since the 1950s, many Jordanian nationals have worked in the Gulf countries, particularly in Kuwait, their numbers growing rapidly in the 1970s and early 1980s. Amman's Ministry of Labor estimated that in 1985 about 340,000 Jordanians were working abroad, largely in the Gulf states; including accompanying family members, expatriate Jordanians numbered from 800,000 to one million.

---

[1] *EIU: Country Report—Syria,* No. 2, 1991, p. 24.

[2] *The Economist,* "A Survey of the Middle East," September 28, 1991, p. 9.

[3] *EIU: Country Report—Syria,* No. 3, 1991, p. 19.

[4] *EIU: Country Report—Syria,* No. 1, 1992, p. 6.

Employment within Jordan in the mid-1980s was about 500,000. In relation to its population, the number of Jordanians working abroad greatly exceeded that of Egypt and Syria, and probably any other Arab country. At the same time, there were, according to official estimates, some 130-140,000 foreigners working in Jordan, mostly Egyptians.[1] Unofficial estimates of foreign workers, including those without work permits, were far higher. The Jordanians abroad were, for the most part, well-paid professionals and skilled workers, while the "imported" workers were largely low-paid manual laborers working in agriculture, construction and some of the services.

On balance Jordan did well in the early 1980s with (net) remittances averaging close to $1 billion *per annum* in 1981-86. For an economy with a GNP of $5.8 billion in 1986, this was a large external infusion.[2] Moreover, the above estimates do not take into account unofficial transfers (not through banks), possibly adding 50-100 percent to total remittances. Grants from the rich Arab states rose strongly following the first oil shock and escalated with the second oil shock. In 1979-82 average annual grants received were almost $1.2 billion, equal to about 30 percent of GNP in those years. Jordan was also the recipient of concessional loans from the Gulf states, the U.S. and other industrialized countries. The rich Gulf states provided a booming market for Jordan's exports, mainly fruits and vegetables and some manufactured products. The Iran-Iraq war (1980-88) was also a boon for Jordan. Once Iran cut off Iraq's access to the Gulf, Jordan became one of the main alternative routes for Iraqi imports from abroad, as well as an important market for Jordan's own products and, until 1988, Iraqi oil exports. The port of Aqaba thrived, and, thousands of trucks were engaged in transporting goods, civilian and military, from Aqaba to Iraq. GDP (in real terms) rose by over 12 percent per annum in 1974-81—8 percent per capita. GNP, which also takes account of remittances, rose even more rapidly. Living standards (measured by the growth in real private

---

[1] *MEED*, August 30, 1986, p. 46; August 1, 1987, p. 16.

[2] See Appendices—Table 8.

consumption per capita) rose by almost 10 percent *per annum*, virtually doubling within seven or eight years.[1]

This period of high level growth and prosperity nearly came to a complete halt in the late 1980s. By 1986-89, grants received had dropped to $500-600 million per annum, less than half the level of the early 1980s, and concessional loans also diminished. The number of Jordanian workers abroad fell only slightly, though declining wage rates in the Gulf states drove down remittances more steeply after 1986. Moreover, as the Iran-Iraq war dragged on and Iraq's financial situation deteriorated, Baghdad restricted imports and fell behind in payments for goods already delivered. As a result, the Central Bank of Jordan was forced to bail out its businessmen by extending credit to Iraq. Both before and since the Kuwait crisis, Iraq had been shipping oil to Jordan for its own consumption, charged to the debt.

Jordan, which had heretofore been fiscally prudent, took many commercial loans in the 1980s. Its civilian external debt (excluding loans to finance arms purchases) rose from $1.4 billion in 1978 to $5.7 billion in 1988, and debt service (annual payments on account of principal and interest) skyrocketed from $129 million to over $1 billion dollars between 1978 and 1988. The ratio of debt service to exports of goods and services (a measure of the burden of the debt) rose from 16 percent in 1985 to a very onerous 28 percent in 1989. In 1988 Jordan defaulted on some loans. By early 1990 the debt had risen to over $8 billion, of which close to $3 billion was attributed to arms purchases abroad.[2]

Amman undertook a sharp devaluation in 1988 and an austerity program followed. The so-called Paris Club of lenders to Jordan rescheduled its debt, and an agreement with the IMF was concluded in April 1989, which included a sharp reduction in food subsidies and in the overall budgetary deficit. Eleven people were killed in subsequent rioting triggered by the steep rise in food prices.[3]

---

[1] See Appendices—Tables 8 and 9.

[2] *Financial Times*, January 23, 1990, p. 6.

[3] *MEED*, February 8, 1990, p. 9.

Domestically, things were going from bad to worse. Between 1981 and 1987, the growth of GDP barely exceeded the increase in population, and living standards dropped by 15 percent between 1983 and 1987.[1] According to official estimates, GDP dropped by 5 percent between 1987 and 1989, or by over 10 percent per capita. In those two years, living standards fell by a devastating 22 percent, according to official estimates, in all falling by one-third between 1983 and 1989. Inflation, which had been modest during the 1970s and 1980s, rose by 26 percent in 1989.[2] According to estimates of a Jordanian economist, inflation was really 10-15 percent higher than indicated by official estimates.[3] In that case, the drop in living standards was even steeper than the official figures indicate.

Possibly the most severe problem facing Jordan was the high rate of unemployment, particularly among university graduates. Between the mid-1970s and the mid-1980s, Jordan had enjoyed full employment. Its rapidly expanding economy and the large exodus of its nationals to work in the Gulf created local shortages which were filled by foreign workers. It was the only non-oil Arab country which had become a large importer of labor; an estimated 175-200,000 foreigners were working in Jordan in 1989, while 328,000 Jordanians were working in the Gulf states.[4] But during the latter half of the 1980s, the recession in the Gulf states, as well as in Jordan, had foreclosed most job opportunities for new university and college graduates, who are averse to accepting the menial jobs performed by the foreigners working in their country.

In January 1990, the Minister of Labor stated that there were 60,000 unemployed; the Prime Minister's estimate was 80,000, while unofficial estimates put the number of unemployed in early 1990 still higher—100,000-120,000. According to the Ministry of Labor, the unemployment rate was 20 percent—and even higher according to independent estimates.

---

[1] See Appendices—Tables 8 and 9.

[2] See Appendices—Table 8.

[3] *EIU: Country Report—Jordan*, No. 3, 1990, p. 4.

[4] *EIU: Country Profile—Jordan—1990-91*, p. 14.

Projections were that by 1995 the number of unemployed Jordanians would reach an even more dangerous level—about 200,000—some one-third of the Jordanian labor force.[1] A British economic journal summarized the situation in 1990 before the Persian Gulf War as follows:

> "The economic situation is so bad . . . that renewed and spontaneous outbreaks of popular unrest cannot be ruled out . . . Jordanians are . . . faced by rising unemployment, high inflation and frozen salaries. There is still bread to eat [due to] subsidies, but few other comforts . . . [F]or the majority there is little prospect of a change . . . for the next five or probably ten years. With popular resentment over past corruption still acute, and with little prospect of a substantive economic improvement, the political situation in Jordan remains explosive."[2]

THE EFFECTS OF THE GULF WAR

The Gulf War seriously aggravated an already depressed economy, especially since Jordan made the costly mistake of siding with Saddam Hussein. Saudi Arabia and the other Gulf states cut off all aid to Jordan, which was nearly half a billion dollars in 1989. The U.S. suspended its aid program, freezing over $100 million. The UN sanctions reduced Jordan's trade (including transit trade) with Iraq. Though this trade had been diminishing since the end of the Iran-Iraq war in 1988, nonetheless it still was almost one-fourth of total Jordanian exports in 1989. The tourist industry, an important sector of Jordan's economy, was adversely affected. But probably the most difficult blow was Kuwait's mass expulsion of Palestinian-Jordanian nationals. 300,000 people had returned to Jordan by the beginning of 1992.[3] Returnees, the Minister of Planning stated, would add some 70,000 to the labor force. Official estimates of the unemployment rate at the beginning of 1992 were 23 percent (unofficial were 35 percent).[4] Remittances for

---

[1] *EIU: Country Report—Jordan*, No. 2, 1990, p. 16; No. 3, 1990, p. 4.

[2] *EIU: Country Report—Jordan*, No. 1, 1990, p. 4.

[3] *EIU: Country Report—Jordan*, No. 1, 1992, p. 4.

[4] *The Middle East*, January, 1992, p. 33.

1991 dropped by $150-300 million, and this probably represents a longer term loss.[1]

1990's GDP was 5.7 percent lower than in the previous year, and in view of the bigger than usual growth in population, per capita GDP dropped by about 15 percent.[2] How much of the decline was due to the burgeoning crisis and how much was a continuation of previous trends is hard to know. One British study estimated that Jordan's losses as a result of the war were $1.8 billion.[3] On the other hand, after the crisis, Jordan benefitted from a large increase in foreign aid, mainly from Japan and Europe, amounting to $1.1 billion.[4] In March 1991 the Finance Minister stated that he expected foreign aid to total $1.36 billion in 1991, well above the $910 million he had projected a few months earlier. At the end of 1990 foreign exchange reserves were $848 million, their highest level since 1982.[5] And in August 1991 the U.S. announced a resumption of civilian aid to Jordan.[6]

For an economy with a GNP of $3.4 billion in 1990, an infusion of $1.4 billion in foreign aid can do much to ameliorate economic problems. Government statistics place the GDP for 1991 at an estimated $4.25 billion.[7] Since the crisis Jordan has suspended payments to some creditors. By mid-1991 it had fallen behind some $500 million in servicing its total $8.3 billion debt.[8] The so-called Paris Club of Western creditors agreed to reschedule its debt of $7.2 billion, giving Jordan additional breathing space. A 1988 order for military aircraft from France, valued at $1 billion, has been canceled,

---

[1] *MEED*, September 20, 1991, p. 23; *The Economist*, October 5, 1991, p. 63.

[2] See Appendices—Table 8.

[3] *EIU: Country Report—Jordan*, No. 2, 1991, p. 14.

[4] *Financial Times*, May 31, 1991, p. 4.

[5] *MEED*, March 29, 1991, p. 7; See Appendices—Table 9.

[6] *MEED*, August 16, 1991, p. 16.

[7] *EIU: Country Report—Jordan*, No. 1, p. 4.

[8] *Wall Street Journal*, June 3, 1991, p. A8.

and this too will help improve Jordan's balance of payments.[1]

But the most difficult problem facing Jordan is massive unemployment, severely aggravated by the Persian Gulf War. More than half of the unemployed are university and college graduates, who had flocked to higher education in the expectation of well-paying jobs in the Gulf states. Kuwait has canceled the work permits of the remaining Palestinians and barred their children from its schools.[2] Nor are they welcome in Saudi Arabia and the other Gulf states. Large-scale foreign aid may help reverse the downtrend in Jordan's economy and economic growth may be resumed in the coming years. But it is hard to see many more productive jobs being created for university graduates within Jordan's economy. Before the war Jordan was urging its unemployed to emigrate and used its influence with the Arab oil states to give its citizens preference over other foreigners. For the most part, that safety valve has been closed. Mass unemployment can be politically and socially destabilizing, especially if it affects the more educated segments of the population.

---

[1] *MEED*, September 6, 1991, p. 22.

[2] *The Economist,* October 5, 1991, p. 63.

VII NON-OPEC OIL PRODUCERS

Leaving aside the countries of the former USSR and the U.S., the world's No. 1 and No. 2 producers respectively, all indications suggest that an oil surplus is in the making. Exploration activity, which had diminished in the mid-1980s, was increasing strongly in the later 1980s with an additional boost from the Persian Gulf War. A survey of twenty large oil companies showed that their capital expenditures for exploration and development worldwide, after falling from $38 billion in 1985 to $24 billion in 1987, rose to $31 billion in 1989. All indicators were pointing towards a continued uptrend even before the Kuwait crisis.[1] Another survey taken in 1989 came to similar conclusions and also noted that "the growing effectiveness of exploratory drilling has helped mitigate the effects of the absolute decline in drilling activity" in earlier years.[2] In other words, new technology has greatly increased the success rate of exploration and lowered its costs. A survey taken following the invasion of Kuwait indicated that oil companies were planning a 14 percent rise in spending in 1991 on exploration and development.[3]

In West Africa, exploration has been expanding rapidly in Nigeria, Cameroon, Gabon, Zaire, and Angola. An American oilman expressed his belief that "hydrocarbon resources (oil

[1] *Financial Times Survey,* November 12, 1990, p. 23.

[2] *Petroleum Economist,* October 1989, pp. 312-314.

[3] *The New York Times,* January 3, 1990, p. D3.

and gas) to be discovered [in West Africa] are large, perhaps even [greater than] the most optimistic forecasts."[1] *Petroleum Intelligence Weekly* reported that drilling in West Africa reached a peak in 1990 and was forecasting a further rise in 1991. Apparently, the oil industry was trying to diversify and expand its sources away from the war-torn Middle East.[2]

Another report (published in May 1991) projected that the pace of exploration in the North Sea in 1991 (largely by the UK and Norway) would be the highest since exploration began thirty years ago, and that 1991 would also see the highest level of production.[3] Output was expected to reach over 4.7 MBD by the mid-1990s, an increase of over one MBD as compared with 1990.[4]

Aside from the North Sea and West Africa many other sectors are reporting new discoveries and expanding oil production. A number of countries have joined the list of oil-producing countries and some have become oil exporters, as their production has exceeded their domestic consumption. None are in the category of giant producers, but their combined effect on oil markets is significant:[5]

1. Angola produced 492 TBD in 1991; this figure is expected to rise to 700 TBD by 1995.[6]

2. Malaysia produced 618 TBD in 1991; this should rise to 800 TBD by 1996-97.[7]

3. Yemen produced 199 TBD in the first half of 1991 and could double its output by 1995.[8] Others are forecasting

---

[1] *Financial Times*, August 2, 1990, p. 22.

[2] *Petroleum Intelligence Weekly*, February 11, 1991, p. 2.

[3] Petroleum Economist and Lloyd's List International, *The North Sea*, May 1991, p. 4.

[4] *Petroleum Intelligence Weekly*, June 10, 1991, p. 2.

[5] This is a partial list, not necessarily in order of importance.

[6] *Petroleum Economist*, January 1992, p. 5.

[7] *Ibid.*

[8] *Ibid.*

production of one MBD by the mid-1990s.[1] In retaliation for Yemen's having sided with Iraq during the Persian Gulf War, Saudi Arabia expelled an estimated 800,000 Yemenis (about one-third of the Yemeni labor force) who had been working there, and also cut off financial aid. Their return to Yemen, and the loss of remittances, which had for many years been its main source of foreign exchange, is a severe blow to Yemen's economy. Yemen is pinning its hopes for recovery on its burgeoning oil revenues.[2]

4. Syrian oil production has risen rapidly in the past few years, reaching a peak of close to 500 TBD in 1991, as compared with 175 TBD in 1985. Syria's Oil Minister has recently spoken of tripling output in the next few years.[3] This is most probably an expression of hope rather than a forecast, but the uptrend is unmistakable.

5. In the past decade Oman has been increasing its output, slowly but surely, from less than 300 TBD in 1980 to a peak of 697 TBD in 1991. The announced goal is 1.0 MBD within the next few years.[4]

6. Brazil projects that production will rise from 638 TBD in the 1991 to one MBD by 1994. The state oil company increased its capital budget by one-third in 1991 in order to achieve its goal.[5]

7. In mid-1991 British Petroleum announced "a significant oil discovery" in Colombia.[6] Colombia's output was 421 TBD in 1991 and will probably rise over the next few years.

8. Despite its lingering communist ideology, Vietnam has also invited Western oil companies to explore and develop its

[1] *Petroleum Intelligence Weekly*, May 13, 1991, p. 3.

[2] *MEES*, October 4, 1991, pp. 4-5.

[3] *EIU: Country Report—Syria*, No. 3, 1991.

[4] *Petroleum Economist*, April 1990, p. 130; November 1990, pp. 5-6.

[5] *Petroleum Intelligence Weekly*, April 22, 1991, p. 3.

[6] *Financial Times*, July 10, 1991, p. 27.

oil resources. It produced 78 TBD in 1991 and expects to reach 200 TBD by 1992 or 1993.[1]

9. In the spring of 1991 an Australian oil company announced a "significant" oil find in Papua New Guinea. Commercial production is expected to begin in late 1992 at an initial rate of 100 TBD.[2]

---

[1] *Petroleum Economist,* January, 1992, p. 5.

[2] *Financial Times,* April 3, 1991, p. 30.

VIII NEW DEVELOPMENT AND EXPLORATION

The oil shocks of 1973-74 and 1979-80 gave a powerful boost to oil (and gas) exploration and development, and after a time lag of a few years there was a significant expansion of world output. Excluding the U.S. and the then-USSR, non-OPEC production rose almost steadily from 7.6 MBD in 1973 to over 16 MBD in 1983, and close to 20 MBD in 1991. **The mini oil shock of 1990-91—the Persian Gulf War—has already given an additional boost to exploration and development, and higher production will almost inevitably follow in the coming years.**

In the 1970s, the standard forecasts of higher oil prices were based in part on projections that world oil reserves would shrink, as new discoveries lag behind extraction. Precisely the opposite occurred. Professor Peter Odell of Holland, one of a handful of dissenters who, in the 1970s and early 1980s, correctly predicted lower rather than higher prices, noted in the spring of 1990 that in the last twenty years over twice as much oil has been added to reserves as has been used. The current world ratio of reserves to production of 42 years is, historically, an all-time high. "Rather than running out of oil—as had been widely feared in the 1970s—the world continues to run into more oil in more and more places."[1] In 1950, the world's proven oil reserves were about 100 billion

---

[1] Peter Odell, Director of the Center for International Energy Studies, Erasmus University, Rotterdam. "The Outlook for Oil Supply and Prices," May 9, 1990, p.5 (on file with the author).

barrels; in 1970, 550 billion barrels; and in 1990, over 1000 billion barrels.[1]

Professor M. Adelman has neatly disputed the widely-held view regarding oil reserves. "Oil reserves are not a one-time stock to be used up, but an inventory always being consumed and replenished by investment in new and especially in old fields."[2] New techniques have made it economically feasible to extract far more oil from old fields. New technology has also made it easier and **less costly** to discover new fields. The drive to explore for and develop these resources had been gathering momentum since the later 1980s, even before the Persian Gulf War. The war gave oil and gas exploration and development an additional push, especially outside the Middle East.

U.S. OIL PRODUCTION

The U.S. is the world's second largest oil producer, 8.9 MBD in 1990, and the largest consumer, 16.2 MBD. The wide gap between production and consumption makes the U.S. the world's leading oil importer—over 7 MBD in 1990.[3] Clearly, any significant change in American production and/or consumption is bound to have a powerful impact on world oil markets.

In 1970, U.S. production peaked at 11.3 MBD and then declined, almost steadily, to 9.7 MBD in 1976. In the following year, Alaskan oil began to flow, and the downtrend was reversed. Production rose slowly until 1985 when it reached 10.6 MBD. This was, again, followed by declines until 1991 when production was down to 8.4 MBD—2.2 MBD lower than in 1985. Towards the end of 1990, the downtrend was, again, reversed. In the first half of 1991, U.S. output was 200 TBD **higher** than in the same period a year earlier, both in Alaska and in the continental U.S.[4] The reversal was attributed

---

[1] *The Economist—Survey of Energy and Environment*, August 31, 1991, p. 7.

[2] M.A. Adelman "The 1990 Oil Shock is Like the Others," *The Energy Journal*, Volume 11, No. 4, 1990, p. 9.

[3] *BP Statistical Review of World Energy*, June 1991.

[4] See Appendices—Table 1.

mainly to a new technique called horizontal drilling which extracts more oil from many older fields.[1] The use of this technique has been increasing rapidly in the U.S. and is being adopted in many other countries. As a result, previously marginal fields have become profitable.[2] To be sure, this does not necessarily portend another longer period of rising U.S. output. The U.S. is the most explored country in the world, and there are powerful pressures on the part of environmental groups against increased exploration and development in Alaska and in other areas. But even if the fall in U.S. output is not fully arrested, a slower rate of decline would have a strong impact on world oil markets.

Domestic political considerations have practically nullified many moves towards more U.S. oil production and, as compared with other industrialized countries, little has been done to restrain consumption. The U.S. Department of Energy believes that theoretically up to 300 billion barrels of oil remain to be recovered from old fields, many of which have been abandoned after only one-third of their oil had been extracted. Moreover, DOE also believes that with appropriate incentives, recovery rates could be substantially improved.[3] There is no indication of any strong move afoot by the administration and the Congress to provide more attractive incentives to substantially increase oil output. However, as noted earlier, some companies have adopted new techniques which have substantially improved recovery rates in existing fields. We shall further discuss U.S. and world oil demand in a later section of this paper.

POST-SOVIET/CIS OIL PRODUCTION

Among the factors contributing to higher prices in 1989 were the strong declines in both American and Soviet production. In 1989, U.S. output fell by almost 600 TBD and Soviet output, which had peaked in 1987-88, dropped by over 300 TBD. Following the invasion of Kuwait in August 1990,

---

[1] *Petroleum Economist,* January 1991, pp. 5-7.

[2] *Petroleum Intelligence Weekly,* April 30, 1990, pp. 2-3.

[3] *Petroleum Economist,* February 1990, pp. 59-62.

over 4 MBD of Iraqi and Kuwaiti oil were removed from international oil markets. At the same time, there was a whopping decline of 725 TBD in Soviet output in 1990. However, while U.S. output seems to have reversed its downtrend since the last quarter of 1990 (at least for the short term), CIS production continued to plunge, as output in 1991 was over 1.0 MBD lower than in 1990. Since its peak in 1987-88, Soviet production dropped by a massive 2.3 MBD—the equivalent of "losing" another Kuwait.

With production of 10.3 MBD in 1991, the Soviet Union remained the world's foremost producer. At the peak in 1987 the Soviets were exporting some 4 MBD, about one-third of their output.[1] In that year Soviet exports of crude and refined oil products exceeded those of any other country including Saudi Arabia. What happens to the post-Soviet oil industry has, and will have, a major impact on world oil markets.

The size of CIS proven reserves remains unknown. British Petroleum estimates that there were 57 billion barrels at the end of 1990 as compared with U.S. reserves of 34 billion barrels.[2] Both CIS and foreign analysts agree that this grossly understates the potential, as vast areas of the CIS remain unexplored. Moreover, an official of the Western Siberian Geology Institute noted in 1990 that of the 489 identified oil and gas fields in Western Siberia only 123 were currently producing.[3] A CIS economist noted that "a whole new source of oil [in] Eastern Siberia and the Arctic Zone [has hardly been touched] . . . If the capital and expertise of [Western oil] companies [were brought in] there is no telling how high production will go."[4] What has happened to the oil industry is part and parcel of the collapse of the CIS economy, communist ideology, and the political system. And some analysts believe

---

[1] *MEES,* September 5, 1988, pp. D1, D2.

[2] *BP Statistical Review of World Energy,* June 1991, p. 2.

[3] *Financial Times,* October 26, 1990, p. 18.

[4] *Forbes,* September 17, 1990, p. 131.

that the oil industry suffers more inefficiencies and technological backwardness than other industries.[1]

During the past few years the authorities in a number of countries that made up the former USSR have sought to attract foreign oil companies to provide the necessary capital and technology needed to develop their oil resources. As of late 1991 a few foreign companies successfully negotiated joint ventures, and many more are in the process of negotiation. The Russian republic (where the bulk of the oil is located) has offered to lift current restrictions limiting foreign firms to 50 percent of joint ventures.[2] The problem appears to be the uncertainty regarding the legal and political system, namely, the struggle between the central government and the republics, and within the republics there are claims of various regional and local governments. The uncertainties as to who owns the oil reserves and what taxes will be imposed by the various levels of government appear to be the major obstacles to foreign investment.[3] Nonetheless, the number of Western companies concluding agreements is rising. Western analysts who have examined the possibilities exude great optimism, some going so far as to suggest that "the (oil) potential of this country is greater than anywhere else in the world."[4] This may well be an exaggeration, but there is every likelihood that there will be far more involvement on the part of Western oil companies, and that within a few years, the downtrend in CIS output will be reversed, with the result that the increase in CIS oil exports, possibly beginning with the mid-1990s, will exert powerful downward pressures on oil prices.

---

[1] *The New York Times*, January 25, 1990, pp. 1, D8.

[2] *Petroleum Economist*, August 1991, pp. 9-12.

[3] *Petroleum Economist* March 1991, p. 52.

[4] *Newsweek*, October 21, 1991, p. 42.

IX OIL DEMAND

While this paper has thus far focussed on the likely future of supply, the picture is not complete without an analysis of likely oil demand.

Changes in oil consumption in a country, or in the world as a whole, depend on three factors: a) the rate of economic growth—measured by changes in real GNP, i.e., corrected for inflation; b) the relationship between changes in real GNP and in consumption of energy from **all** sources; and c) the share of oil within the so-called energy basket.[1] Before 1973, in the U.S. and in the world as a whole, energy consumption rose at about the same rate as economic growth, and oil usage rose even more rapidly, as oil was displacing other sources of energy, especially coal. Oil consumption rose by an annual average rate of 7-8 percent while world economic growth averaged 4-5 percent per annum. The oil shocks of 1973-74 and of 1979-80 radically altered these relationships. **At least two factors have restrained oil demand since 1973. The first is a significant improvement in energy efficiency, with the result that the growth in energy consumption was far smaller, in percentage terms, than that of GNP.** Micro-level examples of these improvements are a decline in the quantum of energy needed to produce a ton of steel, chemicals or other products; less energy usage per unit of cooling or heating; more miles per gallon of gasoline, etc. **The second is that oil has been displaced**

---

[1] More precisely, change in demand equals change in current consumption plus or minus stock changes. Since we are concerned with the longer term, temporary stock fluctuations can be ignored.

by other sources of energy including natural gas, hydro and nuclear power, and coal. In periods of recession, oil demand was also held down by the decline or slow growth of the economy.

Predicting future oil demand over the long run is a hazardous undertaking. Even so, hopefully we can detect the direction of change and some order of magnitude, taking note of historical experience and of new factors which might affect future changes in energy efficiency, and in the share of oil within the energy basket. In the U.S., taking the period 1973-89 as a whole, the average annual rate of growth of energy efficiency was 2.0 percent. "Oil efficiency" (the combined effects of energy efficiency and oil displacement) rose by 2.7 percent per annum. Simply put, the growth in energy usage lagged far behind economic growth, and the use of oil lagged even more, the reverse of long-term trends before 1973. While it might be argued that 1973-89 included the periods of recession which followed the two major oil shocks, an examination limited to the 1983-89 period, which was characterized by favorable rates of economic growth and was recession-free, indicates that while the U.S. economy grew by 3.9 percent per annum during that period, energy consumption rose far less, by 2.3 percent per annum, and oil usage by only 2.0 percent. In other words oil consumption was rising at about half the rate of economic growth, in sharp contrast with the period before 1973 when oil consumption grew far more rapidly than GNP. Moreover, this was a period of sharply declining oil prices in nominal terms, and even more so in real terms. The incentive for fuel switching away from oil was considerably weakened by low oil prices, but was, nonetheless, positive.[1]

In many other industrialized countries the improvement in energy efficiency and in oil displacement was more pronounced. In the Western industrialized countries of the OECD, the amount of oil used per dollar of GNP fell by 40 percent between 1973 and 1985, and by an additional 5-6

---

[1] The sources for the data underlying these calculations are the IMF *International Financial Statistics*, various issues; *BP Statistical Review of World Energy*, various issues; and U.S. Department of Energy *Monthly Energy Review*, various issues.

percent in 1985-88.[1] Japan is a prime example of rapid improvements in energy efficiency and oil substitution. It has been calculated that if the U.S. used oil as efficiently as Japan (per dollar of GNP), its oil consumption in 1989 would have been 9.2 MBD, approximating domestic production. In that case U.S. oil imports would have been approximately zero. In reality U.S. oil consumption was 16.6 MBD and imports were about 7 MBD in 1989.[2]

What about the future? Of the many issues to be considered, the following are most pertinent:

First, a British analyst noted in 1989 that investments made to conserve oil, in the aftermath of the two major oil shocks, are still coming on-stream, including energy-efficient factories, houses, and forms of transport, which will continue to depress demand for oil well into the next century.[3] One might add that the mini-oil shock caused by the Persian Gulf War will, most probably, provide an additional spur to measures designed to improve energy efficiency and oil displacement. While, the U.S. raised the tax on gasoline only marginally, other industrialized countries, including such major oil users as Germany and Japan, which already impose far higher taxes on gasoline and other refined oil products, took advantage of the Gulf crisis to impose additional levies.[4] Higher domestic oil prices will surely stimulate more energy efficiency and oil conservation. In Japan, the world's second largest oil importer, MITI (the Ministry of Trade and Industry), issued a set of recommendations in 1990 designed to improve energy efficiency. If the past is any guide, one can assume that Japanese industry will abide by the guidelines. Toshiba and Hitachi are developing more energy-efficient products including various household appliances; Mitsubishi and others are focusing on superconductivity; and Nippon Steel and

---

[1] *The Economist*, February 4, 1989, pp. 17-19.

[2] *The Economist*, August 25, 1990, p. 15.

[3] *The Economist*, February 4, 1989, pp. 17-18.

[4] *Wall Street Journal*, August 20, 1991, p. 32; *Petroleum Economist*, April 1991, p. 12.

Toyota are working on electric cars.[1] Honda and Mitsubishi announced in 1991 that they would soon be introducing new cars which consume 10-25 percent less gasoline.[2] An example of American industry improving energy efficiency is Boeing. The aircraft manufacturer's new 777 will use only about half of the fuel per seat as the older 727. There are many more examples of new technology improving energy efficiency.[3]

Second, the movement for a cleaner environment—the Greens as they are known in Europe—has been gathering strength; is having a greater influence on governments, firms, and individuals; and strongly urges measures to reduce air and water pollution. According to the U.S. Environmental Protection Agency, the Clean Air Act of 1990 will, over time, reduce U.S. oil consumption by at least 800 TBD.[4] OPEC is increasingly concerned by these developments. At its meeting in June 1991 it adopted a resolution calling on member countries "to exercise greater vigilance in all matters concerned with the environment and particularly to ensure that petroleum does not suffer unfair discrimination in any measures [proposed by the Western countries]."[5]

Third, the current favorite for oil displacement is natural gas. It is far cleaner than oil environmentally, and is not subject to the kind of supply instability and price volatility which has, at times, affected Middle East oil supplies. Despite the rapid growth in oil reserves, discussed earlier, natural gas reserves have grown even more rapidly and are now the equivalent of 80 percent of oil reserves, measured in terms of energy content. Whereas about two-thirds of world oil reserves are located in the Middle East, gas reserves are far more diffused geographically, with the Middle East's share only about one-third. CIS gas reserves, the world's largest, exceed those of the whole Middle East. During the 1980s (1990 as

---

[1] *Financial Times Survey,* December 14, 1990, p. i.

[2] *Wall Street Journal,* August 1, 1991.

[3] *The New York Times,* December 3, 1990, p. A19.

[4] *The New York Times,* September 14, 1990, p. D3.

[5] *MEES,* June 10, 1991, p. A1.

compared with 1980) world energy consumption rose 19.4 percent; natural gas consumption, 37.3 percent; and oil consumption by a mere 4.1 percent.[1] **Natural gas, in other words, was steadily displacing oil.**

In the U.S., price controls and other regulations restricted the availability of natural gas. These were gradually eased in the latter half of the 1980s and abolished in 1989, ending thirty-five years of gas price controls.[2] The result was that U.S. energy consumption rose 9.9 percent between 1986 and 1990; natural gas consumption, 17.4 percent; and oil a mere 3.4 percent.[3]

Looking to the future, new gas pipeline projects from Canada to the U.S., deregulation of the gas industry both in the U.S. and Canada, and environmental pressures, all portend a strong rise in American gas consumption.[4] One estimate is that by the end of this decade gas may displace 3 MBD of U.S. oil consumption.[5] In 1990, over 90 percent of U.S. gas consumption was from domestic sources, and almost all of the imports were from Canada. Gas accounted for 62 percent of home heating in 1990 as compared with 58 percent in 1986, and a continued increase is projected. Analysts now expect that gas will capture most of the market for new electric power stations, while new refinements should popularize gas-powered air conditioners.[6] But despite increased demand, gas prices in 1991 were at a five-year low.[7] *Petroleum Intelligence Weekly* reported that "a dramatic improvement in drilling efficiency largely accounts for a continued surplus in U.S. gas

---

[1] *BP Statistical Review of World Energy,* June 1991.

[2] *U.S. News and World Report,* July 31, 1989, p. 38.

[3] *BP Statistical Review of World Energy,* June 1991.

[4] *Petroleum Economist,* May 1991, pp. 14-15.

[5] *The New York Times,* May 19, 1991, pp. 1F, 6F.

[6] *The New York Times,* December 27, 1990, pp. D1, D2.

[7] *Wall Street Journal,* April 10, 1991, p. A2.

supplies" and projects that this will keep gas prices lower than oil prices.[1]

The one important area where oil products retain an almost complete monopoly in terms of energy use is in transportation fuels, especially gasoline. In 1990, gasoline accounted for 42 percent of total consumption of U.S. oil production; in Western Europe, 25 percent; and in Japan, 21 percent.[2] Three major oil companies—Shell, Mobil and British Petroleum—are working on a method for direct conversion of natural gas into gasoline and diesel fuel.[3] When and if this technology is developed, and proves to be economically feasible, it will powerfully diminish oil demand.

The CIS has, by far, the largest gas reserves, is the world's leading producer, and exports its surplus by pipeline to Europe. Many analysts believe that with appropriate technology far more gas, as well as oil, remains to be discovered. By one estimate, the "untapped" gas reserves in the Soviet Union are equivalent, in terms of energy content, to Saudi Arabia's massive oil reserves.[4] While then-Soviet oil output declined in 1990, gas production rose by 2.4 percent. Western Europe also has gas reserves, particularly in Norway and Holland. A number of West European countries import gas from the CIS, and Italy also imports Algerian gas via an underseas pipeline. In 1990 it signed an agreement with Algeria to increase gas imports by 60 percent.[5] As for demand, a 1989 estimate projected that West European demand for gas in the 1990s will rise by about 3.5 percent per annum, about double the growth rate of the 1980s. Various legal restrictions on gas consumption have been removed, availability has increased sharply, and prices are more competitive as monopoly controls on distribution have been weakened.[6] A 1991 estimate projects a

---

[1] *Petroleum Intelligence Weekly*, November 12, 1990, p. 8.

[2] *BP Statistical Review of World Energy*, June 1991.

[3] *Petroleum Economist*, January 1991, pp. 5-7.

[4] *Wall Street Journal*, August 17, 1990, p. A4.

[5] *MEES*, March 25, 1991.

[6] *Petroleum Economist*, December 1989, p. 370.

somewhat higher growth rate for Western Europe's demand for gas in the 1990s of 3.8 percent.[1]

Overall, the deliverability of natural gas (wellhead and pipeline capacity) to major consumers, mainly North America and Europe, continues to grow with large new projects in the Gulf of Mexico and Mobile Bay, and a continual expansion of pipeline capacity from Western Canada to the U.S.[2] The more rapid growth in natural gas consumption will necessarily restrain oil demand during the 1990s. The "Green" movement and the mini oil shock of 1990-91 can only strengthen this trend.

Interestingly, a number of OPEC members, and others, have been taking measures to increase domestic gas consumption and thus release more oil for export. Others with large reserves of natural gas are making greater efforts to export gas. Qatar, a small oil producer, has a gas field of enormous dimensions, estimated to exceed the reserves of the U.S., and last year concluded an agreement to export liquefied natural gas to Japan.[3] Iran also possesses enormous reserves of natural gas, and is taking measures to increase domestic consumption in order to release more oil for export. In 1990, Iranian gas exports to the Soviet Union were resumed after a lapse of about ten years.[4]

Some analysts have projected that the movement towards a market economy in the countries of the former Soviet Union and in Eastern Europe, will, after a time-lag, stimulate economic growth and higher levels of oil consumption. In the former Soviet Union, oil consumption was more or less flat in 1983-87, dropped by 2.4 percent in 1988-89, followed by a whopping 7.1 percent decline in 1990. This surely reflected the stagnation and the subsequent collapse of much of the Soviet economy. In Eastern Europe oil consumption was stable in

---

[1] *Financial Times*, April 26, 1991, p. 46.

[2] *Petroleum Economist*, August 1991, pp. 9-12.

[3] *The Middle East*, May 1991, p. 33.

[4] *Energy Economist*, 107-1990, p. 13.

1986-89 and then fell by as much as 14 percent in 1990.[1] The latter apparently reflects the impact of economic restructuring and of much higher domestic prices for oil products.

What about future oil demand in the ex-communist countries? Over the years, the very low domestic energy prices in the Soviet Union and in Eastern Europe induced high rates of consumption, and were also a disincentive to Soviet oil production. A market system would necessarily entail a steep rise in energy prices which would induce enterprises and households to adopt measures improving energy efficiency. In 1990, Soviet energy consumption was about two-thirds that of the U.S. while its GNP was possibly one-third or less. In other words it utilized at least twice as much energy per dollar of GNP as the U.S., and the American economy is by no means the most energy-efficient. In varying degrees this applies to Eastern Europe as well, where the effects of future economic growth on oil consumption should be offset by energy saving.[2] In Hungary, World Bank loans are being used to finance investments in energy conservation.[3] As effective government is restored in the former republics of the Soviet Union, the authorities will most likely seek to increase oil exports by substituting, where feasible, natural gas, and will implement measures to improve energy efficiency.[4] Increasing foreign exchange earnings is of crucial importance to economic revival. Moreover, as personal freedoms have been restored, the environmental movement has gathered strength and this implies favoring the utilization of gas rather than oil. **In all, the odds favor lower oil demand in what used to be called the Soviet Bloc, for many more years.**[5]

Those analysts who project higher oil prices base their predictions, in part, on more rapid growth in oil consumption in the so-called Less Developed Countries (LDCs). This broad

---

[1] *BP Statistical Review of World Energy,* June 1991.

[2] *The Economist—Survey of Energy and the Environment,* August 31, 1991, p. 14.

[3] *Petroleum Economist,* January 1990, pp. 19-21.

[4] In the recent past, well over half of Soviet export earnings were derived from oil.

[5] *The Economist—Energy and Environment,* August 31, 1991, p. 14.

grouping, sometimes called the Third World, includes all countries other than the Western industrialized countries (OECD) and what used to be called the communist bloc (largely the former USSR, China, and Eastern Europe). Within this group of countries some have enjoyed rapid economic growth, mainly the so-called Asian Tigers (South Korea, Singapore, Taiwan, and Hong Kong, joined in the last few years by Thailand and Malaysia), while many other LDCs suffered from economic stagnation. While oil consumption fell in the OECD countries between 1980 and 1985, in the LDCs there was a small rate of growth—2.2 percent per annum. Between 1985 and 1990 OECD oil consumption rose slowly, by 1.7 percent per annum; in the LDCs the growth rate was far more rapid, averaging 4.6 percent per annum. For the 1980s as a whole, oil consumption in the LDCs rose by 3.4 percent per annum.[1]

As noted earlier a good number of countries have recently discovered oil, or have significantly expanded their oil production. Brazil, Argentina and some other Latin American countries, and others, are in this category. In the oil-producing LDCs, OPEC and non-OPEC alike, substantial efforts are being made to restrain local oil consumption by raising domestic fuel prices and by utilizing the associated gas emitted together with oil extraction, much of which is flared. Many LDCs, including oil-producing countries and others, suffer from large external debts and persistent balance of payments deficits and are making efforts to reduce or restrain oil imports, often by raising excise taxes on oil products, or by imposing higher customs duties on oil imports.

It appears likely that the growth rate of oil consumption in the LDCs in the 1990s will continue to be higher than in the OECD countries, who are far more technologically advanced in terms of improvements in energy efficiency and in oil displacement. This in turn is dependent on the answers to a series of questions: But how much higher? Will the more enterprising LDCs, the Asian Tigers and others, follow the lead

---

[1] *BP Statistical Review of World Energy,* June 1991; The definition of LDCs used in this publication which excludes the OECD countries and the former Soviet Union, China, Eastern Europe, Cuba, Mongolia, Laos, North Korea and Vietnam has been applied in this paper. If China were added to the LDCs the rate of growth of oil consumption would be about the same.

of the OECD countries, in particular, Japan, and undertake stronger measures to improve energy efficiency and oil substitution? (The more successful East Asian countries look to Japan as their model for economic development and are likely to adopt and adapt Japanese machinery and equipment, vehicles, consumer appliances, and so forth, which are superior in terms of energy efficiency.) Will environmental pressure groups in the LDCs have a stronger impact on oil consumption? To what extent will the experience of the Persian Gulf War influence these countries to change their energy policies and reduce oil imports? The rapid economic growth of a number of East Asian countries, and a few other LDCs, based in large measure on growing exports to the OECD countries, has stimulated rising oil consumption. But will this pace of export-led economic growth continue in the 1990s? Will the OECD countries impose greater restrictions on imports from these countries? The expanding European Common Market and the emerging North American Common Market may add obstacles to imports from non-members of these clubs. There are many imponderables and no certain answers to these questions. Simply extrapolating from the past has often led to erroneous conclusions, and those who do so today may be repeating past errors. **One can surmise that in the 1990s LDC oil consumption will rise more rapidly than that of the OECD, but the rate of growth may well decelerate.**

WORLD OIL DEMAND

The pertinent factor in assessing oil markets is total world supply and demand. In 1990, LDCs accounted for 24 percent of world oil consumption, the OECD 57 percent, and the former Communist Bloc 19 percent. The LDCs may well continue to increase their consumption more rapidly than others, but in all likelihood at a slower rate than in recent years. In the OECD countries, oil consumption fell drastically (18 percent) between 1979 (when it reached a peak) and 1983. Subsequently, there was a slow rate of growth in OECD oil consumption, averaging 1.4 percent per annum between 1983 and 1990, resulting from the rapid recovery from the serious recession of the early 1980s combined with strongly declining oil prices. In the 1990s, an average annual growth rate of 1-1.5 percent will be an **upper limit** for OECD oil consumption. And in fact it may well be lower in view of continuing technological changes in energy efficiency, the displacement of oil (especially by natural gas), the growing impact of environmentalism, and the aftermath of the mini oil shock caused by the Persian Gulf War. As for the ex-communist countries, oil demand may well continue to decline for many more years, for reasons discussed earlier, offsetting, at least in part, the higher growth rate of oil demand in the LDCs.

Following world oil consumption's 12 percent drop between 1979 and 1983, it rose by 1.6 percent per annum between 1983 and 1990. In 1990 it was still below its 1979 peak. **In all, world oil consumption in the 1990s will not rise by more than 1-2 percent per annum, and very possibly less.**[1] The impact of the mini oil shock occasioned by the Kuwait crisis will be a smaller growth in demand than what it might have been had there been no crisis.[2]

---

[1] Professor Peter Odell forecast—before the Persian Gulf war—that oil demand in the 1990s would rise by 1.2 per annum. Peter Odell, Director of the Center for International Energy Studies, Erasmus University, Rotterdam. "The Outlook for Oil Supply and Prices," May 9, 1990.

[2] See *Financial Times,* October 18, 1990, p. 14.

X THE OUTLOOK FOR OIL MARKETS AND PRICES IN THE 1990s

Before Iraq's invasion of Kuwait, most oil analysts projected that prices would climb in the 1990s in real terms, i.e., over and above dollar inflation. Oil demand, it was believed, would rise by 1.0 MBD per annum, and non-OPEC output would at best be stable. Thus dependence on OPEC, and especially the Gulf producers, would rise, and OPEC in turn would exploit the opportunity to raise prices.[1] OPEC's own projections were that the cartel's production of 22.6 MBD in 1989 would reach 30 MBD by the end of the decade, based on the assumption that non-OPEC production would decline.[2] One research center, assuming more rapid growth in oil demand and a decline in non-OPEC production capacity, concluded that "it is virtually inevitable that [during the 1990s] world demand will outstrip OPEC's preferred capacity (author's note: *whatever that means*) implying growing market power for OPEC producers."[3] By 1995, it was said, the price of oil would rise to $25 per barrel in real terms.[4] Another energy specialist concluded that by the end of the century prices would rise to $30-35 per barrel,

---

[1] *Financial Times Survey—World Oil Industry*, November 12, 1990, p. 23.

[2] *Middle East Review 1990*, London, p. 19.

[3] *Petroleum Economist*, January 1990, pp. 24-28.

[4] *Forbes*, May 14, 1990, p. 40.

measured in 1988 dollars,[1] which in current dollars would mean $48-56 per barrel.[2]

To be sure there were dissenting views, including those of this author.[3] An analysis of oil markets in *The Economist* (April 1990) noted that the Green movement was stimulating conservation, that prospects for long-term oil supplies looked good, that gas reserves were soaring, that OPEC was expanding capacity by 6 MBD by the mid-1990s, and that non-OPEC production would rise steadily throughout the decade. It concluded that "real oil prices are more likely to fall than rise [in the 1990s]."[4]

After the invasion of Kuwait some analysts contended that little had changed in terms of long-term forecasting. Non-OPEC output will level off, they argued, and demand for OPEC oil will rise more rapidly.[5] In 1991, the International Energy Agency projected that by the end of the decade real oil prices would reach $30, measured in 1986 dollars, i.e., $52 per barrel in current dollars.[6] These forecasts assumed that oil markets would return to the *status quo ante bellum*, after a brief hiatus.

A study done in the spring of 1991, entitled "The Aftermath: New Forces Unleashed in Middle East Oil

---

[1] *MEED*, February 9, 1990, p. 15.

[2] This assumes that dollar inflation will be 4 percent per annum, which was the rate of inflation in 1985-90.

[3] See Eliyahu Kanovsky, *OPEC Ascendant? Another Case of Crying Wolf*, Policy Paper No. 23, (Washington D.C.: The Washington Institute for Near East Policy, 1990). The paper was published before the invasion of Kuwait.

[4] *The Economist*, April 21, 1990, p. 81.

[5] Petroleum Industry Research Foundation "The Impact of the Persian Gulf Crisis on the Oil Industry," November 1990.

[6] *The Economist—Survey of Energy and the Environment*, August 31, 1991, pp. 1-36; Here again, this assumes that dollar inflation would average 4 percent per annum in the 1990s, similar to the 1985-90 rate of inflation.

Policy,"[1] noted that fourteen Middle East and North African producers accounted for 55 percent of the world's oil imports in 1989, and possessed 70 percent of the world's proved oil reserves, it then concluded that "the Kuwait crisis revealed to all. . . that the Middle East and North African exporters have the capacity to dominate world oil trade for as long as we can see into the future." Furthermore, it was argued, the Kuwait crisis showed that the OECD countries "could absorb prices up to $25 with very little impact on economic growth and oil demand." The author noted that the Persian Gulf War and its aftermath significantly increased revenue requirements of a number of Persian Gulf oil exporters, and concluded that they will raise prices to satisfy these needs. Since an oil price of $25 will not, he argued, adversely affect oil demand in the industrialized countries, or have recessionary effects on their economies (reducing oil demand) the exporters will utilize their (presumed) power to raise prices to the $25 level.

The reasoning underlying these conclusions appears to be faulty. Sellers do not have the power to raise prices because they "need" more money; and prices are determined by total supply and demand forces. **Even a monopolist has limitations with respect to price setting, and OPEC is not a monopoly.** Nor would the "new OPEC" (the fourteen Middle East and North African oil exporting countries) have any more power than the present cartel. Cartels are by their very nature fragile. **The inducement to "cheat" on agreed upon prices or production quotas is even more powerful when financial needs are greater.** This has been the history of OPEC agreements since quotas were first agreed upon in 1982. Of course, only those with spare capacity were able to "cheat." But the very large growth in production capacity in various OPEC countries planned for the 1990s that was discussed earlier, some of which is already in the process of implementation, and the more powerful inducement to overproduce to finance much higher public expenditures, bode ill for the existing OPEC cartel, or for any new cartel envisioned by the author of the above study. Interestingly enough, a study published in the *OPEC Review* in the spring of 1991 expressed the view that the

---

[1] Henry Schuler, Director, Energy Security Programs, Center for Strategic and International Studies, Washington, D.C., May 1, 1991 (on file with the author).

financial needs of members of OPEC and their announced plans to expand capacity will induce many to expand output (beyond their quotas) and thereby depress prices.

Writing in the *Wall Street Journal* (December 10, 1990) a Saudi economist stated: "I'm not worried about $60, $80 or $90 per barrel oil (as some were predicting during the height of the Kuwait crisis). I'm worried about the price falling to $12 or $14. Saudi Arabia is almost certain to object to a cutback in its output." He then went on to list others, in particular, Venezuela, UAE and Iran, who also raised their output strongly since the crisis and would balk at any future reductions.

Since the Persian Gulf War, more analysts have reached the conclusion that (real) oil prices are heading downward. The chief economist at one of the larger American oil companies believes that since the Persian Gulf War the long-term trend line has shifted downward by as much as $3-5 per barrel. He has predicted that the new real price of oil (measured in 1990 dollars) will be $15-20 for the next 10-20 years.[1] Similarly an analyst at the World Bank reached the conclusion that the world is now in an era of low energy prices.[2] Shortly after the invasion of Kuwait and the abrupt cutoff of Kuwaiti and Iraqi oil, *The Economist* projected that the major industrialized countries would increasingly prefer oil from outside the Gulf, and favor natural gas and more conservation. The rise in prices following the invasion "will result in a much longer term glut [after the crisis] leaving OPEC even more impotent."[3]

A study published in September 1991 arrived at even more far-reaching conclusions, namely that the long-term price of oil would be $9 per barrel (in 1990 prices). The author's reasoning was that:

"In the future, the growth in consumption of refined oil products will be hampered by fuel efficiency and environmental initiatives designed to substitute natural gas for oil in utilities and vehicles . . . the fundamentals point to excess crude supply . . . technology improvements continue to lower the cost of drilling

[1] *Wall Street Journal*, April 29, 1991, pp. A3, A8.

[2] *World Bank News*, April 11, 1991.

[3] *The Economist*, August 18, 1990, pp. 65-66.

and exploration, while developing countries seek foreign investment (to explore for and develop their oil and gas resources) by offering equity production or reduced taxes. Overall, costs (of oil exploration and development) are declining. The fundamentals in place—slower growth in oil demand, coupled with excess production capacity and lower operating costs—will combine to cause prices to decline."[1]

All of the issues raised in this passage have already been dealt with here in greater detail. Our chief focus, however, is on the worsening financial situation of the Gulf countries as a consequence of the war and their far stronger drive to increase production capacity in order to expand exports. The experience of the two previous oil shocks has made them leery of high oil prices. They fear that significantly higher prices would soon be followed by an oil glut, and that going through another boom and bust cycle would be nothing less than calamitous for the major oil-exporting countries.

OPEC is in a dilemma. Its leading members need much higher oil revenues. Raising prices—if they could succeed in raising them—would soon boomerang on them as it did in the 1980s. They are aware of the large increase in oil supplies in the pipeline which may cause a glut and depress prices, especially when Kuwait and Iraq reenter the markets full blast. OPEC has, therefore, decided to seek the "cooperation" of the major oil-consuming countries to "stabilize" the market. There is no doubt that if the OPEC countries felt that the price trends were upwards and in their favor they would see no need for "consultations" with buyers. (No consultations were sought by OPEC following the two major oil shocks.) At the behest of OPEC, twenty-five oil exporting and oil consuming countries convened in mid-1991. At the meeting, the Secretary-General of OPEC asserted: "Experience has demonstrated repeatedly that the oil market will not look after itself."[2] In other words, oil markets must be regulated and controlled. Since OPEC does not possess the necessary power, it is seeking the help of the main oil buyers to forestall a major drop in prices. Wisely, the U.S. did not participate in this thinly-disguised attempt at price-fixing.

---

[1] *Petroleum Economist*, September 1991, pp. 41-43.

[2] *Financial Times*, July 3, 1991, p. 25.

XI SUMMARY AND CONCLUSIONS

1. The Persian Gulf War and its aftermath have significantly raised the revenue requirements of Saudi Arabia and the UAE—hence their determination to expand production capacity and capture a larger share of world oil markets.

2. Kuwait's financial needs for reconstruction are enormous. The decline in its foreign assets as a result of the war implies that investment income will be significantly lower. In other words, its dependence on oil revenues has risen very strongly and it, too, will seek to expand capacity beyond its pre-war level. OPEC restrictions will have even less of an effect on Kuwait's oil policies than before the war.

3. One cannot say when UN sanctions on Iraqi oil exports will be lifted. But when they eventually are, Iraq will go all out to restore and then expand its oil production and exports. When Iraq invaded Kuwait, its economy was just beginning to emerge from the disastrous effects of the eight-year war with Iran. It will take many, many years to restore the Iraqi economy, even with competent political leadership, and it is utterly dependent on oil revenues to achieve its goals. If reparation payments are enforced, Iraq will have to produce and sell even more oil.

4. In the short run, Iran gained from the higher prices prevailing since the Persian Gulf War. But it is still licking its wounds from the ruination caused by the 1979 revolution and the 1980-88 war with Iraq. It has announced major plans for reconstruction and development and a large expansion in oil production capacity. It will need every penny of oil revenues, and more, to achieve its goals.

5. A number of other OPEC members, in particular Venezuela, Libya and Nigeria, are planning increases in production capacity.

6. **An oil glut is in the making.** This is in part a consequence of the Persian Gulf War, which has given added stimulus to oil exploration worldwide, while demand has become more sluggish. OPEC appears to be aware of this and is seeking the "cooperation" of the major oil-importing countries. At a meeting of twenty-five oil importing and oil exporting countries in July 1991, the Secretary General of OPEC stated that "experience has demonstrated repeatedly that the oil market will not look after itself."[1] In other words, competitive markets may be desirable elsewhere but not for oil. During earlier periods of sharp price increases in the 1970s and early 1980s, when oil prices shot up and most analysts were predicting still higher prices, OPEC did not seek the "cooperation" of the oil buyers. The U.S. did not attend the July 1991 meeting, and hopefully will continue to oppose price rigging. For the U.S. and other buyers lower oil prices would be a boon to the economy.

7. OPEC's ability to sustain, let alone raise, prices has never been strong in periods of an oil glut. We can anticipate that the announced plans calling for a major expansion of production capacity both in member and non-member countries will, for the most part, be implemented. Before the war many analysts argued that the expansion plans announced by a number of OPEC members would be constrained by capital shortages. The increased oil revenues obtained by the oil exporters during and since the war have removed or at least eased this constraint. **Whether OPEC continues to exist, in a formal sense, is immaterial; its power to determine prices will be further emasculated by the coming oil glut.** Moreover, while before the Persian Gulf War, the fear of Iraqi and possibly Iranian military or terrorist actions may have had some restraining effect on OPEC members' volume of production, i.e., the degree to which they would violate their OPEC quotas, no such external restraint is currently visible on the horizon.[2]

---

[1] *Financial Times*, July 3, 1991, p. 25.

[2] Wars and revolutions in major oil-producing countries can raise prices, but the experience of the Persian Gulf War indicates that the price hikes would be of relatively small magnitude as compared with earlier

8. During the last few years, oil prices were sustained by major declines in output in the U.S. and USSR, the world's leading oil producers. In the U.S., the long-term outlook is for a smaller rate of decline. In the former Soviet Union, the change in policy favoring investment by Western oil companies will probably reverse the downtrend within the next few years. Some analysts are even more optimistic, predicting an oil boom in the Soviet Union.

9. Excluding the U.S. and the CIS, non-OPEC output is likely to rise. The large increase in exploration and development activities reported by the Western oil companies, and the new technology which has increased the success rate of exploration, and has lowered costs, presage a continued expansion of non-OPEC production. Whereas in the 1970s nationalization of the foreign oil companies was the vogue in Third World countries, there has been a complete reversal in recent years. These countries, as well as the ex-communist states, are offering tempting inducements to Western companies to invest their capital and utilize their advanced technology to develop their oil and gas resources. This policy greatly enhances the probability of success. The Persian Gulf War gave added stimulus to exploration activities outside the volatile Persian Gulf area. **In other words, dependence on Persian Gulf supplies may well diminish.**

---

oil shocks. The Strategic Petroleum Reserve is one tool available in dealing with such an eventuality, but there are many more. U.S. policy should favor a greater diversification of suppliers with preference for less volatile areas than the Persian Gulf. Middle East oil is widely regarded as "cheap." While this may be the case with respect to the costs of production, as the head of the Venezuelan oil company stated shortly after the invasion of Kuwait: "When you (the U.S.) are buying the cheap oil of the Middle East, you're not calculating the cost of defending the Middle East." Back in 1988 the U.S. National Defense Council estimated the cost of oil-related defense outlays in the Persian Gulf region at about $14 billion, which works out to $29.50 per barrel of oil imported from that area. In effect, Japanese and West European importers of oil from the Persian Gulf region are getting a subsidy of $8.2 billion a year, at the expense of the U.S. taxpayer. (*The Washington Post,* July 29, 1990.) This has wide implications, but insofar as oil is concerned, a greater diversification of oil supplies would be a wise and prudent policy. One way of doing this is by strengthening the World Bank facility which lends to the less developed countries for projects designed to increase domestic energy sources and also provides them with the tools and know-how to conserve energy.

10. On the demand side, there is ample evidence that energy efficiency continued to improve even in 1983-89, a period of declining oil prices. New technologies were and are being developed and adopted, which presage further improvements. The growing environmental movement in the industrialized countries, and more recently in the ex-communist countries, give added impetus to this trend. Increasingly, abundant and cheap natural gas supplies, which are both environmentally superior and less costly, are displacing oil.[1] The Persian Gulf War has given added stimulus to this trend. Whereas some two-thirds of the world's proved oil reserves are in the Middle East, only one-third of natural gas reserves are located in that region. About 90 percent of American gas consumption is from domestic sources and almost all the rest is from Canada. Europe, including the Soviet Union, requires no imports from outside the region.[2]

In sum, the underlying long-term trend points to lower oil prices, at least in real terms, and possibly even in nominal terms. It is well to recall that during the first half of 1990, i.e., before the invasion of Kuwait, the price of the "OPEC basket" (a weighted average of OPEC oil prices) had declined by some 25-30 percent to $14. It may well return to that level. This does not rule out fluctuations due to weather, accidents, wars and revolutions. But market forces would subsequently restore

---

[1] However, as compared with Japan and various West European countries, the U.S. has been laggard. These countries impose oil import fees and/or far higher taxes on gasoline and other oil products, thereby promoting energy efficiency and fuel switching away from oil. In the aftermath of the Persian Gulf War, Germany and Japan and others again raised taxes on oil. In the U.S. such measures appear to be politically taboo. The Secretary of Energy noted (in 1991) that in real terms the price of gasoline has never been cheaper, and added, probably in a moment of frustration, that the American public believes that "the Bill of Rights gave them unleaded regular for $1.06 a gallon and they better get it or . . . they'll get the bums out of office." (*The New York Times*, March 4, 1991, p. D3.) Perhaps if it were labeled "The Persian Gulf Oil Defense Tax" it would have a better chance of acceptance, especially if the Japanese and Europeans contributed their shares. Such measures would stimulate both oil conservation and a greater diversification of oil supplies, further reducing the shocks that might emanate from any future turmoil in the Persian Gulf.

[2] Italy imports gas from Holland, the Soviet Union and Algeria. It could well increase its imports from the other sources if Algerian gas were not available.

prices to their underlying trend. Technology will continue to improve energy efficiency and erode the importance of oil. New sources of oil from a growing number of non-OPEC countries will further undermine the power of OPEC to set prices. The Middle East oil exporters will struggle, like the others, for market shares.

These trends have important ramifications for oil importing countries, both rich and poor. For them, lower oil prices mean less inflation, lower interest rates, more rapid economic growth, jobs and incomes. **On the other hand, those economies heavily dependent on oil export revenues will face difficult problems.**

STATISTICAL APPENDICES

TABLE 1. OIL PRODUCTION

TABLE 2. SAUDI ARABIA—Balance of Payments

TABLE 3. SAUDI ARABIA—Budgets

TABLE 4. SAUDI ARABIA—Selected Economic Indicators

TABLE 5. EGYPT—Balance of Payments

TABLE 6. EGYPT—Budgets

TABLE 7. EGYPT—Selected Economic Indicators

TABLE 8. JORDAN—Selected Economic Indicators

TABLE 9. JORDAN—External Accounts

TABLE 10. SYRIA—Selected Economic Indicators

TABLE 11. SYRIA—External Accounts

TABLE 1. Oil Production (millions of barrels per day)

	1977	1978	1979	1980	1981	1982	1983	1984	1985	1986	1987	1988	1989	1990	1991
Saudi Arabia	9.2	8.3	9.5	9.9	9.8	6.5	4.5	4.1	3.2	5.0	4.2	5.2	5.2	6.5	8.2
Kuwait	2.0	2.1	2.5	1.7	1.1	0.8	1.1	1.2	1.0	1.4	1.3	1.4	1.8	1.2	.191
Iraq	2.3	2.6	3.5	2.6	0.9	1.0	1.1	1.2	1.4	1.7	2.1	2.7	2.8	2.1	.297
UAE	2.0	1.8	1.8	1.7	1.5	1.2	1.1	1.1	1.2	1.4	1.5	1.6	1.9	2.1	2.3
Qatar	0.4	0.5	0.5	0.5	0.4	0.3	0.3	0.4	0.3	0.3	0.3	0.3	0.4	0.4	.381
Libya	2.1	2.0	2.1	1.8	1.1	1.1	1.1	1.1	1.0	1.0	1.0	1.0	1.1	1.4	1.4
Algeria	1.2	1.2	1.2	1.1	1.0	1.0	1.0	1.0	1.0	0.9	1.0	1.0	1.1	1.2	1.2
Iran	5.7	5.2	3.2	1.5	1.3	2.4	2.4	2.0	2.2	1.9	2.3	2.2	2.9	3.1	3.24
Mideast OPEC	24.9	23.8	24.3	20.8	17.2	14.4	12.6	12.0	11.4	13.7	13.6	15.4	17.2	17.9	14.7
Total - OPEC	31.3	30.0	31.0	27.0	22.7	19.3	17.8	17.5	16.4	18.7	18.3	20.4	22.6	23.9	22.3
Total - World	61.9	63.4	65.8	62.8	59.3	56.6	56.5	57.7	56.9	59.9	59.9	62.3	63.8	64.3	62.9
of which:															
U.S.	9.9	10.3	10.1	10.3	10.2	10.2	10.2	10.5	10.6	10.2	9.9	9.8	9.2	8.9	8.4
USSR	11.0	11.5	11.8	12.1	12.2	12.3	12.4	12.3	12.0	12.4	12.6	12.5	12.2	11.5	10.3
Non-OPEC excluding U.S. and USSR	9.8	11.7	12.8	13.6	14.2	14.7	16.1	17.3	18.0	18.6	19.1	19.6	19.8	20.1	19.6

Sources:
Petroleum Economist, London, Monthly

Notes:
1. The figures for Saudi Arabia and Kuwait include their shares of the Neutral Zone.
2. Middle East OPEC is defined here as the seven Arab members of OPEC, listed in the table, plus Iran.

TABLE 2. Saudi Arabia: Balance of Payments-Selected Data (billions of dollars)

	1974	1975	1976	1977	1978	1979	1980	1981	1982	1983	1984	1985	1986	1987	1988	1989	1990
Exports Merchandise (FOB)	30.1	27.3	35.6	40.4	37.0	58.1	100.7	111.9	73.9	45.7	37.4	27.4	20.1	23.1	24.3	28.3	44.3
Exports Services	2.6	3.3	4.6	6.1	6.5	7.7	11.3	16.0	19.0	20.2	17.6	16.1	13.9	13.1	12.8	12.7	2.5
Total Exports	32.7	30.0	40.3	46.4	43.5	65.8	112.0	127.9	92.8	65.9	55.0	44.0	34.1	36.3	37.1	41.0	56.0
Imports Merchandise (FOB)	3.6	6.0	10.4	14.7	20.0	23.5	25.6	29.9	34.4	33.2	28.6	20.4	17.1	18.3	19.8	19.2	21.5
Imports Services	4.6	6.5	11.2	14.4	18.9	24.3	33.7	45.8	41.1	40.3	36.0	27.6	21.0	19.5	15.4	21.0	23.4
Private Transfers- Workers' Remittances	0.5	0.6	1.0	1.5	2.8	3.4	4.1	5.3	5.3	5.2	5.3	5.2	4.8	4.9	6.2	6.6	11.6
Total Imports	8.7	13.1	22.6	30.6	41.8	51.1	63.3	81.0	80.9	78.7	69.8	53.1	42.9	42.7	41.4	46.8	56.5
Official Transfers (Foreign Aid)	1.0	3.1	3.3	3.9	3.9	3.5	5.9	5.7	4.4	4.0	3.6	3.2	3.0	3.3	2.5	2.2	4.4
Balance on Current Account	23.0	14.4	14.4	12.0	-2.2	11.2	42.8	41.1	7.6	-16.9	-18.4	-12.9	-11.8	-9.8	-6.8	-8.1	-4.1
Foreign Assets of Central Bank (End of Year)	22.0	38.7	51.2	59.4	60.0	61.7	86.8	126.5	137.7	125.3	109.7	87.7	73.7	68.9	63.3	60.5	
Net Foreign Assets of Banking System (End of Year)	22.2	39.2	52.3	61.4	61.7	64.8	93.7	139.4	153.7	141.2	126.3	104.2	93.1	89.7	86.3	83.0	

Sources:

International Monetary Fund, *International Financial Statistics*, various issues

Notes:

1. Merchandise exports are dominated by oil. The figures include re-exports.
2. Service exports are dominated by investment income. They also include income from tourism, mainly from Muslim pilgrims.
3. Service imports include payments to foreign contractors. They apparently include some military imports.
4. The foreign aid figures apparently exclude so-called loans to Iraq during the Iran-Iraq War in 1980-1988, and some other loans to other Arab countries.
5. Since much of the aid to Iraq, and aid to some other Arab countries was in the form of loans, they are included in the foreign assets held by the central bank. In other words, the foreign assets of the central bank (and of the banking system) are, realistically, much lower than shown in the table.

TABLE 3. Saudi Arabia: Budgets (billions of dollars)

	1974-75	1975-76	1976-77	1977-78	1978-79	1979-80	1980-81	1981-82	1982-83	1983-84	1984-85	1985-86	Annualized 1986	1987	1988	Provisional 1989	Provisional 1990
Total Revenue	28.4	29.3	38.5	37.9	39.3	63.0	104.9	108.2	71.7	59.5	48.4	36.6	26.0	31.3	22.6	30.6	31.5
of which: Oil	26.8	26.5	34.3	32.7	34.4	56.5	96.2	96.6	54.2	41.8	29.3	16.8	12.8	16.1	12.9	20.3	20.2
Investment Income	1.2	2.2	3.2	3.3	3.0	4.4	6.4	8.9	14.0	13.5	9.0	6.3	5.7	4.8	3.2	2.9	2.9
Special Transfers from Oil Companies											4.3	7.1	2.1	4.6			
Other	0.5	0.6	0.9	1.9	1.9	2.1	2.2	2.7	3.5	4.1	5.8	6.4	5.4	5.8	6.5	7.4	6.6
Total Expenditures	10.0	23.2	30.2	39.3	43.7	56.2	71.3	83.7	71.4	66.3	61.1	50.4	45.7	49.5	36.0	38.7	38.1
of which: Projects	5.6	12.3	15.5	19.1	19.2	31.2	37.1	42.8	36.3	23.8	22.5	14.7	11.8	15.4	6.8	7.1	8.2
Operations and Maintenance										7.7	7.3	6.6	6.1	6.1	5.3	5.0	5.0
Military	2.5	6.7	9.0	9.1	10.6	16.9	16.5	19.3	19.4	18.5	19.3	16.7	13.9	14.1	12.8	12.8	13.8
Foreign Aid	0.8	1.2	2.4	3.2	1.9	2.9	7.4	7.1	4.0	3.7	3.0	3.0	2.6	3.1	2.0	1.7	1.7
Other	1.0	3.0	3.3	8.0	11.9	5.3	10.3	14.5	11.7	12.6	9.1	9.4	11.2	10.8	9.1	11.3	4.8
Balance	18.5	6.1	8.3	-1.4	-4.4	6.8	33.6	24.5	0.4	-6.8	-12.7	-13.8	-19.7	-18.2	-13.4	-8.1	-6.6

Sources:
Saudi Arabia Monetary Agency, *Annual Reports*
Middle East Economic Digest, various issues
Economist Intelligence Unit: Saudi Arabia—Country Reports and *Country Profile*

Notes:
1. All the figures are actual revenues and expenditures, except for 1989 which are provisional.
2. Until 1985-86, the fiscal years were based on the Muslim calender. Since 1987 the fiscal years approximate the common calender. 1986 was a transition year of less months. The figures for 1986 in the table are annualized.
3. Investment income is from public sector deposits held in the central bank. The bulk of these deposits is held abroad.
4. Special transfers from the state owned oil companies, Aramco and Petromin, began in fiscal 1984-85 and ended in 1987. These profits had previously been retained by the oil companies to finance further investment in the oil sector.
5. Other revenues consist mainly of customs duties and various fees. These have been raised in recent years in order to reduce the budgetary deficit.
6. The projects budget consists mainly of investment by the public sector in infrastructure. Until fiscal 1983-84 the budget for operations and maintenance of the infrastructure was included in the projects budget.
7. There are various off-budgetary expenditures consisting of some arms imports, so-called loans to Iraq, and others.

TABLE 4. Saudi Arabia: Selected Economic Indicators (billions of dollars unless indicated)

	1972-73	1973-74	1974-75	1975-76	1976-77	1977-78	1978-79	1979-80	1980-81	1981-82	1982-83	1983-84	1984-85	1985-86	1987	1988	1989	1990
Gross Domestic Product (GDP)	10.9	28.0	39.7	46.6	58.2	66.3	74.3	156.5	155.1	121.1	107.7	99.7	86.7	73.2	73.6	76.1	83.0	
Budgetary Balance— Surplus or Deficit (-)	0.9	5.6	18.5	6.1	8.3	-1.4	-4.4	6.8	33.6	24.5	0.4	-6.8	-12.7	-13.8	-19.7	-18.2	-13.4	-15
Ratio of Budgetary Balance to GDP-%	8.3	20.0	46.6	13.1	14.3	-2.1	-5.9	4.3	21.7	20.2	0.4	-6.8	-14.6	-18.9	-26.8	-23.9	-16.1	
Military Expenditures	0.9	1.5	2.5	6.7	9.0	9.1	10.6	16.9	16.5	19.3	19.4	18.5	19.3	16.7	13.9	14.1	12.8	
Ratio of Military Expenditures to GDP %	8.3	5.4	6.3	14.4	15.5	13.7	14.3	10.8	10.6	15.9	18.0	18.6	22.3	22.8	18.9	18.5	15.4	

Calendar Years	1973	1974	1975	1976	1977	1978	1979	1980	1981	1982	1983	1984	1985	1986	1987	1988	1989	1990
Value of Oil Exports Crude plus Refined	7.8	35.6	29.6	38.5	43.5	37.4	58.6	101.4	111.5	73.3	42.8	34.3	24.2	17.0	19.3	20.2	24.1	40.28
Balance on Current Account Surplus or Deficit (-)	2.5	23.0	14.4	14.4	12.0	-2.2	11.2	42.8	41.1	7.6	-16.9	-18.4	-12.9	-11.8	-9.8	-7.7	-8.5	-4.11
Arms Imports	0.1	0.3	0.3	0.6	1.3	1.5	1.4	1.8	2.9	3.2	4.0	3.4	3.9	3.8	5.5	3.0		

Sources:

See Tables 2 and 3.
U.S. Arms Control and Disarmament Agency *World Military and Arms Transfers 1989* and earlier issues

Notes:

1. Military expenditures in this table are from the budgets, and the ratio of military expenditures to GDP is based on official figures. Unofficial sources indicated that there are off-budgetary military outlays. See, for example, Stockholm International Peace Research Institute, *SIPRI Yearbook 1990*, p. 197, which estimates the ratio of expenditures to GDP For most years, the latter estimates are higher, sometimes significantly higher than those based on Saudi official estimates.

2. The figures for arms imports are from the U.S. Arms Control and Disarmament Agency. The Saudis do not publish estimates of their arms purchases.

3. The balance on current account of the balance of payments refers to exports of goods and services minus imports of goods and services and foreign aid.

TABLE 5. Egypt: Balance of Payments (millions of dollars)

	1974	1975	1976	1977	1978	1979	1980	1980-81	1981-82	1982-83	1983-84	1984-85	1985-86	1986-87	1987-88	1988-89	1989-90	1990-91
Exports (FOB) *of which:*	1672	1567	1610	2042	2170	2951	4085	3985	4144	3555	4033	3833	3236	2580	3098	2820	3276	4216
Oil	187	315	622	696	915	1878	2997	2857	3032	2468	2640	2589	2027	1225	1385	1148	1299	2158
Other Goods	1485	1252	988	1346	1255	1073	1088	1128	1112	1087	1393	1294	1209	1360	1712	1672	1927	2058
Imports (CIF)	3512	4799	4370	4715	5300	6987	8988	9063	8978	9040	10287	10516	9527	7952	9838	10277	10774	11381
Exports-Services *of which:*	709	1080	1975	2550	3457	4080	5340	3609	3606	3962	3968	3982	3824	4445	4849	5389	5920	6913
Tourism	265	332	464	728	704	601	773	512	393	304	288	410	315	380	886	901	1067	689
Suez Canal Dues	—	84	311	428	515	589	663	780	909	957	974	897	1028	1148	1269	1307	1472	1536
(Plus) Remittances	188	366	755	897	1767	2214	2696	2855	2082	3166	3930	3497	2973	3012	3384	3522	3744	3427
Import-Services	497	723	815	1090	1425	1522	2168	2991	3477	3460	3915	4308	4511	4068	4178	4718	5204	6603
Official Transfers	994	986	624	445	346	89	97	—	51	791	772	1097	1209	974	698	756	1110	4656
Balance on Current Account	-593	-1400	-890	-768	-751	-1389	-1634	-1605	-2572	-1026	-1499	-2365	-2786	-1005	-1987	-2499	-1928	1228
Foreign Exchange Reserves	214	177	216	402	481	529	1046	—	688	698	739	736	792	829	1378	1263	1520	2683
Foreign Debt	4415	7870	10049	13684	17164	18573	21490	24331	26481	28611	29822	31920	37122	39440	40425	43100	46100	
Arms Imports	230	350	150	270	350	600	625	775	1900	1400	1100	1500	1200	1700	725	600		

Sources:

National Bank of Egypt, *Economic Bulletin*, various issues
International Monetary Fund, *Balance of Payments Yearbook*, various issues and *International Financial Statistics*, various issues
U.S. Department of Agriculture, various publications
U.S. Arms Control and Disarmament Agency (ACDA), *World Military Expenditures and Arms Transfers 1989*

Notes:
1. Since 1980 the fiscal year begins July 1.
2. The figures for foreign exchange reserves and the foreign debt are for the end of the calendar years, i.e., 1981-82 refers to the end of 1981.
3. The figures for tourism and workers' remittances are probably underestimated since much is channelled through the black market.
4. The Suez Canal was reopened in mid-1975. It had been closed since 1967.
5. Official transfers refer to grants from other countries. In addition there were loans from various countries, many on concessional terms.
6. The balance on current account refers to exports of goods and services (including workers' remittances), plus private and official transfers, minus imports.
7. Gold reserves, not shown in the table, have been a steady 2.432 million ounces throughout this period.
8. Figures for the foreign debt may well exclude some or all of the debt incurred in arms imports. The estimates for arms imports are from ACDA.

TABLE 6. Egypt: Budgets (millions of Egyptian pounds, current pounds)

	1974	1975	1976	1977	1978	1979	1980-81	1981-82	1982-83	1983-84	1984-85	1985-86	1986-87	1987-88	1988-89	1989-90	1990-91
Total Domestic Revenues	1184	1524	2015	2755	3306	3684	7363	8323	9749	10371	11312	12792	13499	15983	18307	20093	28226
Total Expenditures	1989	2912	3280	4074	5445	6591	9892	13259	14497	16804	18476	20526	21237	26832	30155	34691	47832
of which:																	
Subsidies	410	622	434	650	710	1352	2168	2909	2142	2876	2749	2766	2270	2737	3325	4659	4737
Military	314	303	453	343	339	772	1065	1475	1683	2120	2385	2646	2784	2986	3389	3832	4170
Overall Deficit	805	1388	1265	1319	2139	2907	2529	4936	4748	6433	7165	7734	7738	10849	11847	14559	19605
Foreign financing(net)	119	210	488	513	767	628	612	818	858	1052	1530	1796	1831	2499	2963	3097	13898
Net Deficit	686	1178	776	806	1372	2279	1917	4118	3890	5381	5634	5938	5907	8350	8885	11501	5708
GDP (current prices)	4190	5247	6705	8210	9788	12618	17149	20881	24834	27886	32516	36039	45249	54553	64688	79300	93600
GNP (current prices)	4085	5099	6572	8643	10771	13395	18462	21327	26051	30605	35892	39397	46818				
Ratios in Percentages:																	
Overall Deficit/GDP	19.2	26.5	18.9	16.1	21.9	23.1	14.7	23.6	19.1	23.1	22.0	21.5	17.1	19.9	18.3	18.4	20.9
Net Deficit/GDP	16.4	22.5	11.6	9.8	14.0	18.1	11.2	19.7	15.7	19.3	17.3	16.5	13.1	15.3	13.7	14.5	6.1
Subsidies/GDP	9.8	11.9	6.5	7.9	7.3	10.7	12.6	13.9	8.6	10.3	8.5	7.7	5.0	5.0	5.1	5.9	5.1
Military Expend./GDP	7.3	5.8	6.8	4.2	3.5	5.8	6.2	7.1	6.8	7.6	7.3	7.3	6.0	5.5	5.2	4.8	4.5
Military Expend./GNP	7.4	5.9	6.9	4.0	3.1	5.8	5.8	6.9	6.5	6.9	6.6	6.7	5.8				
Military Expend./GNP (ACDA)	35.7	31.9	23.9	22.8	16.0	12.5	9.5	9.1	15.2	13.4	13.7	12.8	11.5	11.5	8.6	5.0	

Sources:

National Bank of Egypt, *Economic Bulletin*, various issues

International Monetary Fund, *Government Financial Statistics Yearbook* and *International Financial Statistics*

Economist Intelligence Unit: Country Report, various issues

U.S. Arms Control and Disarmament Agency (ACDA), *World Military Expenditures and Arms Transfers 1989*

Notes:

1. The data include both the central government and local government units as well as transfers in both directions between the Ministry of Finance and state enterprises.

2. In some years the Ministry of Finance assumes responsibility for the debts of state enterprises to the banks. Hence, the year-to-year changes in government outlays may not be very meaningful.

3. The figures for the subsidies refer to explicit direct subsidies for food and some other necessities such as public transportation. Implicit subsidies such as for energy are believed to be even larger than explicit subsidies.

4. Transfers of profits from state enterprises (mainly oil and Suez Canal) are recorded in the budget at the "official" exchange rate. In other words, their contribution to state revenues is understated. On the expenditure side, state imports of food and other "necessities" are recorded in the budget at the official exchange rate. In other words, the recipients of these products benefit from an implicit as well as explicit subsidy.

5. Net foreign financing refers to loans received in a given year minus repayments in that year.

6. In 1980 a fiscal year beginning July 1 was adopted. Available data for calendar year 1980 are incomplete.

7. Military expenditures are clearly understated in the announced budget. Arms exports are apparently off-budget. Moreover, there are reports that the armed forces have additional sources of income, not included in the budget. See, for example, *Middle East Economic Digest*, January 24, 1987, p. 5. The estimates of Egyptian military outlays published by the U.S. Arms Control and Disarmament Agency (ACDA) are invariably higher or far higher than those noted in the budget as is clearly evident from the accompanying table.

TABLE 7. Egypt: Selected Economic Indicators

	1974	1975	1976	1977	1978	1979	1980	1980-81	1981-82	1982-83	1983-84	1984-85	1985-86	1986-87	1987-88	1988-89	1989-90	1990-91
Crude Oil Output-Millions of Metric Tons		11.7	16.6	20.8	24.8	26.5		31.0	32.5	34.5	39.1	43.7	42.6	44.0	44.9	43.5	44.4	45.1
Domestic Oil Consumption-Millions of Metric Tons		7.4	8.1	8.6	9.3	10.4		11.9	13.4	15.3	16.8	17.9	17.2	18.4	18.9	18.6	19.3	19.4
Tourist Nights-Millions		5.9	6.8	6.4	7.1	7.1		9.3	9.6	9.0	8.7	9.0	8.2	11.8	15.7	18.4	22.1	
Index of Real private Per Cap. Consumption (1984-85=100)	58.3	63.1	67.1	68.7	76.6	90.3		89.0	97.6	96.1	98.2	100	88.6	102.2	100.4	98.2		
Annual % changes in Real Gross Domestic Product	5.1	14.3	7.2	7.9	10.1	8.7		10.0	5.5	6.4	6.0	12.1	9.1	6.4	6.2	5.3	5.8	
Annual % change in Value-added in Industry	6.0	6.2	6.8	6.8	5.5	7.9	9.0	8.8	5.5	7.4	8.8	9.9	7.4	7.3	7.2	7.3	7.3	
Index of Agric. Production (1979-81=100)	91.4	91.3	94.7	92.5	95.2	99.5	100.6	99.7	105.1	106.4	106.9	113.3	119.0	124.9	124.5	128.9		
Above-Per Capita	106.8	105.5	105.7	100.6	100.7	102.3	100.6	97.0	99.5	98.0	95.9	98.8	101.0	103.2	100.2	101.1		
Agric. Exports—Millions of Dollars	982	782	734	823	664	606	677	741	673	726	756	662	669	662	728			
Agric. Imports—Millions of Dollars	1206	1417	1377	1547	1997	1668	2350	3636	3217	3304	3942	3840	3623	3545	5143			
Agric. Trade Balance—Millions of Dollars	-224	-635	-643	-724	-1333	-1062	-1673	-2895	-2544	-2578	-3186	-3178	-2954	-2883	-4415			
Annual % Change in Implicit Price Deflator	6.3	7.4	19.2	13.5	8.2	18.6	20.7	20.5	10.3	11.8	11.5	4.0	1.6	18.0	13.6	12.6		
Annual % Change in Consumer Price Index	10.0	9.7	10.3	12.7	11.1	9.9		10.3	14.8	16.1	17.0	12.1	23.9	19.7	17.7	21.3	16.8	
Annual Percentage Change in Wholesale Price Index	14.3	7.5	7.8	9.3	14.8	9.7	21.7	8.0	9.3	16.0	10.0	13.2	17.3	13.7	26.3	27.3	16.8	

Sources:

National Bank of Egypt, *Economic Bulletin*, various issues
International Monetary Fund, *International Financial Statistics*, various issues
U.S. Department of Agriculture, various publications

Notes:

1. As noted earlier, since 1980, the fiscal year begins July 1. The national accounts follow the fiscal year. Figures for 1980 are incomplete. There are some series which are on a calendar year basis. In this table the figures for agriculture—all from the U.S. Department of Agriculture—are on a calendar year basis. This is also the case with respect to the consumer and wholesale price indices. In these series the figures under the heading 1980-81 refer to calendar year 1981, and so on.

2. Tourist nights refers to the number of tourists multiplied by the number of nights at hotels in Egypt.

3. The index of real private per capita consumption was calculated by deflating the estimates for private consumption in the national accounts, given in current prices, by the official consumer price index, and then calculating per capita real consumption based on the population estimates published in the IMF International Financial Statistics. If, as is commonly believed, the official consumer price index understates inflation, the decline in living standards in the latter half of the 1980s is even more pronounced.

4. Until 1973 the agricultural trade balance had been positive, i.e., agricultural exports exceeded agricultural imports. Since 1974 there has been a persistent deficit reaching a record $4.4 billion in 1988.

5. The official estimates of real growth in GDP are disputed by independent sources. The latter believe that inflation is underestimated and, hence, real growth is overestimated. See *Economist Intelligence Unit: Country Report—Egypt*, No. 2, 1991. No index of industrial production was found. The estimates for value added are from the national accounts.

TABLE 8. Jordan: Selected Economic Indicators

	1974	1975	1976	1977	1978	1979	1980	1981	1982	1983	1984	1985	1986	1987	1988	1989	1990
GDP in Constant 1985 Prices—Index, 1985=100	38.9	43.8	53.1	56.5	64.9	67.8	79.7	87.6	92.4	94.8	96.1	100	109.2	112.9	114.3	107.8	101.7
Above—Per Capita	60.4	65.2	75.7	77.1	84.9	85.6	96.8	102.2	103.8	102.3	99.8	100	105.4	105.2	102.9	93.9	78.5
Index of Agric. Production—1979-1981=100	102.9	74.6	80.5	82.9	104.3	76.2	113.4	110.3	107.0	134.8	122.4	148.3	130.3	154.1	160.3	145.0	
Above—Per Capita	132.2	90.7	94.3	93.2	113.0	79.7	113.3	106.9	99.8	121.5	106.0	122.9	103.9	118.2	118.4	103.0	107.5
Index of Industrial Production 1985=100	26.4	28.3	35.4	36.7	45.1	54.0	64.4	75.1	77.6	81.5	93.4	100	101.4	110.8	101.8	106.1	
Index of Real Private Per Cap Consumpt.-1985=100	50.2	56.3	60.1	63.7	71.6	86.0	85.2	96.7	99.1	107.2	103.0	100	96.1	91.4	86.8	71.6	72.9
Gross Fixed Capital Formation/GDP (%)	21.0	23.2	26.9	32.2	29.8	32.2	33.3	39.9	37.2	31.7	28.4	24.0	20.8	19.7	18.9	18.3	20.0
Total Consumption /GNP (Ratio)	1.06	98.5	85.3	85.9	90.2	1.05	91.0	91.2	93.3	1.07	1.09	1.11	1.05	1.04	1.04	0.98	1.27
Mil. Expend./GNP (%)	35.1	29.5	42.6	31.9	27.9	29.6	23.3	21.1	20.1	19.8	19.5	19.7	14.2	13.9	21.0	12.7	
Consumer Price Index-1985=100	39.6	44.4	49.5	56.7	60.6	69.3	77.0	82.9	89.0	93.5	97.1	100	100	99.8	106.4	133.8	155.4
Implicit GDP Price Deflator—Index-1985=100	41.1	46.1	51.3	58.8	63.0	71.8	79.8	85.9	92.3	97.0	102.4	100	98.4	97.4	101.5	124.1	133.0
Population (Millions)	1.7	1.8	1.9	2.0	2.1	2.1	2.2	2.3	2.4	2.5	2.6	2.7	2.8	2.9	3.0	3.1	3.5

Sources:

Central Bank of Jordan, *Monthly Statistical Bulletin*, various issues,
International Monetary Fund *International Financial Statistics*, various issues
U.S. Department of Agriculture, various publications
U.S. Arms Control and Disarmament Agency *World Military Expenditures and Arms Transfers 1989*, earlier issues
Economist Intelligence Unit: Country Report and Country Profile, various issues

Notes:

1. The index of real private consumption per capita was derived from the official estimates for private consumption in current prices using the consumer price index and the population estimates. It gives us an approximation of changes in living standards.

2. The "investment effort" is measured by the ratio of gross fixed capital formation to GDP.

3. The ratio of total (public plus private) consumption to GNP provides us with a measure of gross national saving. For example, if the ratio is 0.95 the rate of gross national saving is 5 percent. If the ratio exceeds one it implies that gross national savings is negative.

4. The ratio of military expenditures to GNP is from the U.S. Arms Control and Disarmament (ACDA). Their estimates are significantly higher than those derived from the published budgets. They apparently exclude arms imports, noted in Table 2.

Table 9. Jordan: External Accounts (millions of dollars unless otherwise noted)

	1974	1975	1976	1977	1978	1979	1980	1981	1982	1983	1984	1985	1986	1987	1988	1989	1990	1991
Exports—Merchandise (FOB)	154	153	207	249	297	402	575	733	752	580	752	789	732	933	1007	1109	1066	1100
of which:																		
Agricultural Products	38	40	73	89	94	152	200	240	201	145	135	122	136	121	97		59.8	
Exports—Services	125	262	384	483	624	819	1129	1360	1317	1298	1232	1268	1159	1350	1461	1278	1562	
Imports—Merchandise (FOB)	430	648	908	1125	1339	1743	2136	2815	2879	2700	2473	2427	2158	2400	2419	1882	2283	2600
of which:																		
Agricultural Products	168	186	301	304	382	465	525	630	674	612	620	574	579	580	580			
Imports—Services	179	303	402	444	675	1051	1173	1499	1489	1287	1492	1477	1391	1577	1695	1299		
Private Transfers	82	172	402	421	468	509	667	922	933	924	1028	846	984	743	800	565		
Official Transfers (Grants)	251	409	353	500	337	1057	1313	1260	1034	795	688	740	634	599	552	613		
Balance on Current Account	3	45	36	-16	-288	-6	374	-39	-333	-391	-265	-261	-40	-352	-294	385		
Agricultural Trade Balance	-130	-146	-228	-215	-288	-313	-325	-380	-473	-467	-485	-452	-443	-459	-483			
Arms Imports	80	80	140	110	170	100	260	1100	850	1100	230	600	450	350	450	190		
External Debt (Civilian)	287	385	537	897	1359	1692	2366	2788	3175	3674	3972	4294	4936	5360	5650			
Debt Service	16	25	40	70	129	215	352	483	428	570	500	745	811	920	1042	1063		
Foreign Exchange Reserves	297	444	456	627	869	1138	1107	1049	848	798	500	399	413	413	110	460	848	824
Gold Reserves (Thousands of Ounces)	787	787	787	806	811	816	1021	1067	1080	1090	1060	1061	1064	1002	743	748	753	777
Exchange Rate—Dollars Per Jordanian Dinar (Annual Averages)	3.11	3.14	3.01	3.04	3.27	3.33	3.35	3.03	2.84	2.76	2.60	2.54	2.86	2.95	2.69	1.75	1.51	1.053

Sources:
See Table 8.

Notes:
1. Private transfers in these accounts refers mainly to net workers' remittances, i.e., the transfers of Jordanians working abroad to Jordan, minus the transfers out of the country of foreigners working in Jordan. These remittances may be viewed as the export of labor services rather than a unilateral transfer as presented here.
2. Official transfers refers to grants received, largely from the rich Arab states. In addition, there were concessional loans.
3. The external debt as presented here does not fully include debts incurred as a result of arms purchased abroad. It was officially stated in 1989 that the external debt was really about $8 billion in 1988 rather than $5.6 billion as shown in the table. See *Financial Times*, January 23, 1990, p. 6.

TABLE 10. Syria: Selected Economic Indicators

	1974	1975	1976	1977	1978	1979	1980	1981	1982	1983	1984	1985	1986	1987	1988	1989	1990
Index of Real GDP—1985=100	55.4	67.1	73.1	72.1	77.1	81.0	87.8	96.1	98.9	100.7	94.2	100	95.5	96.9	94.8	110.8	107.3
Above—Per Capita	79.1	93.1	97.2	92.3	97.1	98.8	103.6	109.6	109.2	107.7	97.5	100	92.4	90.8	93	86.4	63.68
Index of Agric. Prod.—1979-81=100	70.3	71.3	81.8	76.8	88.0	82.8	106.3	110.8	117.3	117.2	100.2	109.2	118.9	103.2	139.4		
Above Per Capita	86.3	84.6	93.8	85.2	94.4	85.9	106.6	107.4	109.9	106	87.6	92.2	96.9	81.2	105.8	63.2	
Crude Oil Prod.—Millions of Tons	6.4	9.6	10.0	9.1	8.9	8.7	8.3	8.6	8.2	8.5	8.6	8.8	9.8	11.9	14.1	18.3	20.3
Index of Prod. in Manufacturing—1985=100	42	45	54	55	56	57	67	78	92	101	109	100	99	98	93		
Index of Real Private Consump. Per Cap.—1985=100	94.4	104.8	103.7	103.5	119.2	133.0	136.7	157.9	124.7	125.5	110.0	100	86.1	72.3	79.3		
Gross Domestic Investment/GDP Percentages	24.8	28.7	31.4	35.5	27.4	26.2	27.5	23.2	23.7	23.6	23.7	23.8	23.3	18.4	15.9		
Ratio of Budgetary Balance to GDP—%	-8.4	-7.5	-15.6	-8.9	-9.1	0.8	-9.9	-5.0	-9.2	-9.5	-14.8	-13.7	-11.3	-2.0	1.3	-1.3	
Ratio of Military Expenditures to GDP-% (Syrian Accounts)	10.5	15.9	14.6	14.5	14.7	15.9	17.2	14.4	15.6	15.4	15.9	15.6	13.5	10.9	7.4	17.2	14.2
Above—U.S. Arms Control and Disarmament Agency	10.4	15.8	14.6	14.3	14.6	15.9	17.2	14.6	15.8	21.8	22.7	21.8	17.9	11.5	10.9		
Implicit Price Deflator—1985=100	34.6	36.9	40.7	45.0	50.1	57.8	70.2	82.2	83.6	87.4	96.1	100	126.3	158.0	202.5	325.3	388.4
Consumer Price Index—1985=100	29.9	33.3	37.1	41.6	43.6	45.6	54.4	64.4	73.6	78.1	85.3	100	136.1	217.0	292.0	325.3	388.4
Wholesale Price Index—1985=100	33.1	35.6	39.9	43.5	49.1	53.4	61.3	73.0	81.0	83.4	90.8	100	140.5	206.1	301.2	342.9	419.6

Sources:

Central Bank of Syria, *Quarterly Bulletin*, various issues
International Monetary Fund, *International Financial Statistics*, various issues
U.S. Arms Control and Disarmament Agency, *World Military Expenditures and Arms Transfers 1989* and earlier issues
U.S. Department of Agriculture, various publications

Notes:

1. The index of GDP in constant 1985 prices and population estimates used for calculating per capita GDP are from Syrian official sources, published in *International Financial Statistics*.

2. The index of agricultural production is from the U.S. Department of Agriculture.

3. Real private consumption per capita was calculated by correcting the estimates for private consumption in current prices in the national accounts, using the official consumer price index and population estimates.

4. The ratio of gross domestic investment to GDP is based on the official national accounts in current prices. Unfortunately no separate estimates are given for fixed capital formation and the change in stocks.

5. The ratio of the budgetary balance to GDP is based on the current price estimates. The balance is calculated net of receipts of foreign grants.

6. The ratio of military expenditures to GDP is from the budget. It does not include arms imports.

7. The second estimate of military expenditures to GDP is from the above publication of the U.S. Arms Control and Disarmament Agency. Since 1983 ACDA's estimates are significantly higher than those published in the budgets. Both sources excludes arms imports. The latter are given in the following table.

TABLE 11. Syria: External Accounts (millions of dollars)

	1974	1975	1976	1977	1978	1979	1980	1981	1982	1983	1984	1985	1986	1987	1988	1989	1990
Exports—Merchandise (FOB)	783	930	1066	1070	1061	1648	2112	2212	2002	1918	1834	1856	1037	1357	1348	2812	4217
of which:																	
Oil	431	654	671	621	665	1187	1662	1661	1523	1332	1176	1220	561	703	591	1182	1903
Agricultural	264	192	257	311	280	309	276	236	291	279	412	206	237	173	179		470
Exports—Services	310	385	314	383	310	430	456	525	509	575	542	685	576	625	685	710	725
Imports—Merchandise(FOB)	1039	1425	2102	2402	2204	3055	4010	4404	3636	4024	3687	3946	2363	2226	1986	1821	2376
of which:																	
Oil	45	108	195	277	323	822	1068	1728	1501	1357	1402	1153	492	490	165	92	-62
Agricultural Products	383	364	349	335	443	459	588	795	587	913	781	766	498	427	452		520
Imports—Services	397	503	505	454	601	605	600	925	934	1001	1034	1114	836	1149	1097	1477	1650
Private Transfers	44	52	53	93	636	901	774	436	411	387	321	350	323	334	360	355	200
Official Transfers	416	684	402	1143	782	1627	1520	1848	1398	1302	1229	1212	759	762	536	206	800
Balance of Current Account	167	93	-772	-167	-15	946	251	-308	-250	-844	-794	-958	-504	-298	-151	784	1916
Foreign Exchange Reserves	456	685	271	476	374	565	315	266	185	43	263	80	144	273	191	127	163
External Debt (Civilian)	539	736	1110	1681	2326	2734	3364	3303	3360	3465	3523	4201	4527	4645	4860	3315	3357
Debt Service	78	113	120	120	297	410	517	530	532	479	467	516	521	523	658	1073	
Arms Imports	825	380	625	825	1200	2100	3300	2600	2600	3500	2200	1600	1200	1900	1300	1000	
Oil Trade Balance	386	546	476	344	342	365	594	-67	22	-25	-226	67	69	213	426	1090	1467
Agricultural Trade Balance	-119	-172	-92	-24	-163	-150	-312	-559	-296	-634	-369	-560	-261	-254	-273		-50

Sources:
See Table 10.

Notes:
1. The figures for oil exports and imports include both crude oil and refined oil products.
2. Private transfers consist mainly of workers' remittances. Much of the latter is transferred through the black or free market and does not appear in the published balance of payments.
3. Official transfers refer to grants received largely from the rich Arab oil states. These figures apparently also include the value of the annual oil grant from Iran—about one million tons, during most of the years in the 1980s when Iran persuaded Syria to close the oil pipeline from Iraq. These grants, as well as additional oil supplies at discounted prices and long-term credit arrangements, were supposed to compensate Syria for its losses arising from the closure of the pipeline from Iraq.
4. In addition to foreign exchange reserves, Syria has gold reserves of 833 thousand ounces. These have been unchanged since 1979.
5. The foreign debt excludes arms imports, mainly from the Soviet Union, sold on the basis of long-term credits. According to unofficial sources the military debt reached $15-19 billion in 1988. Also excluded from the foreign debt estimates in the table are debts to Iran of about $2.3 billion for oil shipments, noted above. See *The Middle East Review 1989*, p. 156.
6. The official figures for the balance of payments exclude arms imports. The estimates are from the U.S. Arms Control and Disarmament Agency.

RECENT PUBLICATIONS OF THE WASHINGTON INSTITUTE

Democracy and Arab Political Culture—A Washington Institute Monograph by Elie Kedourie

Peace Process Briefing Book—An authoritative guide to the Arab-Israeli peace process with maps and documents

GulfWatch Anthology—A collection of day-by-day analyses of the Gulf crisis by the scholars and associates of The Washington Institute

From War to Peace in the Middle East?—Proceedings of The Washington Institute's 1991 Annual Policy Conference featuring Richard Haass, Dan Meridor, Les Aspin, Ze'ev Schiff and Hanna Siniora

Islam and the U.S.: Challenges for the 1990s—Proceedings of The Washington Institute's 1992 Annual Soref Symposium

After the Storm: An American Strategy for the Postwar Middle East—The interim report of The Washington Institute's Strategic Study Group

Security for Peace: Israel's Minimal Security Requirements in Negotiations with the Palestinians by Ze'ev Schiff

POLICY PAPERS SERIES

Policy Paper 29: *King Hussein's Strategy of Survival* by Uriel Dann

Policy Paper 28: *The Arrow Next Time?: Israel's Missile Defense Program for the 1990s* by Marvin Feuerwerger

Policy Paper 27: *Palestinian Self-Government (Autonomy): Its Past and its Future* by Harvey Sicherman

Policy Paper 26: *Damascus Courts the West: Syrian Politics, 1989-1991* by Daniel Pipes

Policy Paper 25: *Economic Consequences of Peace for Israel, the Palestinians, and Jordan* by Patrick L. Clawson and Howard Rosen

Policy Paper 24: *The Future of Iraq* by Laurie Mylroie

POLICY FOCUS SERIES

Policy Focus 19: *Hamas: The Fundamentalist Challenge to the PLO* by Clinton Bailey

Policy Focus 18: *Baghdad Between Shi'a and Kurds* by Ofra Bengio

Policy Focus 17: *The Arab States and the Arab-Israeli Peace Process: Linkage or Disengagement?* by Barry Rubin

Policy Focus 16: *Towards Middle East Peace Negotiations: Israeli Postwar Political-Military Options in an Era of Accelerated Change* by Dore Gold

For a complete listing or to order publications, write or call The Washington Institute for Near East Policy, 1828 L Street, NW, Suite 1050, Washington, D.C. 20036 Phone (202) 452-0650, Fax (202) 223-5364